CRISIS

AND

CALM

Canada's Central Bank
From Dot-Com 2000 Through
2020 Covid Lockdown

GREG QUINN

 FriesenPress

One Printers Way
Altona, MB R0G 0B0
Canada

www.friesenpress.com

ISBN
978-1-03-916377-5 (Hardcover)
978-1-03-916376-8 (Paperback)
978-1-03-916378-2 (eBook)

1. POLITICAL SCIENCE, PUBLIC POLICY, ECONOMIC POLICY

Distributed to the trade by The Ingram Book Company

TABLE OF CONTENTS

CHAPTER ONE

Why should you read this book? Why did I write it?

This book documents a remarkable yet little-examined time for Canada's economy and the people who manage it. Starting with the Y2K bug and dot-com boom, it moves through the "Great Moderation" of inflation, the 2008 global financial crisis and the Covid recession of 2020. Through this period, Canada's dollar hit record highs and lows and borrowing costs plunged to nearly zero. Bad times during the Covid-19 pandemic were at risk of becoming another Great Depression without massive intervention that was unthinkable in the early 1930s.

This book examines how Canada's central bank did in good times and bad, and what lessons we can draw for the future. While former Bank of Canada Governors have written books, few have directly touched on their own work, and there has been little such outside scrutiny of monetary policy. I argue there are two main and radically different phases of monetary policy in Canada through this era: the relatively smooth and stable management in normal economic cycles, and the far riskier moves needed in times of crisis. While the Bank has been effective most of the time, and arguably more than its peers in the U.S., Japan and Europe, there are several key issues for making Canada's actions better in the future. I also look at proposals being made for big policy changes, which experience suggests would turn out badly.

I wrote this book because I have been an eyewitness to a fertile period of economic history. The year 2000 included the Y2K bug, when people feared early computer programmers had left all the world's computers unable to process the number 2000 in dates, crashing the banking system and the economy. I stayed up through midnight in Washington, just to learn of a minor report that an ATM broke down in South Korea.

In 2001, there was a stock market crash following the dot-com stock bubble, followed by the horrific 9/11 terror attacks on New York and Washington.

After was a return to economic expansion known as the "Great Moderation," a period in which policy makers were lulled into believing the expansion could run without limits, even as so-called financial market imbalances crept up.

This era came with warnings that while growth and inflation remained modest, there was no longer enough demand to push interest rates back up to where they were in past economic cycles. This left many central banks stuck with relatively low interest rates and inflation that would hamstring efforts to help when it was needed in 2008 and 2009. That was the time of the "Great Recession" or the "Global Financial Crisis," during which collapses in banking and housing markets in the U.S. and Europe roiled the global economy. Canada avoided most of the direct damage and suddenly became a poster child for sound policy. Mark Carney became a "rock star" as the first foreigner to run the Bank of England, the most storied of central banks.

Canada's economic good fortune turned into flirtation with a housing bubble, as the ratio of household debt to after-tax income rose above where it was in the U.S. before their crash. Instead of Canada being turbocharged by corporate tax cuts, low interest rates and a sound banking system, corporate Canada went into a torpor as China and Mexico grabbed market share in the U.S.

This resulted in a wobbly and unbalanced economy going into 2020, when the dark times of the Covid-19 pandemic brought severe lockdowns that unleashed the biggest recession since the Great Depression.

This prompted Canada to dig deep into an emergency monetary policy toolkit for the first time, and the government brought in the biggest deficit, as a share of GDP, since World War II. The International Monetary Fund showed this was potentially the biggest fiscal relief plan among major economies in 2020, until Joe Biden seemed to do us one better.

I sat down to write this during the Covid lockdowns. My late grandmother on my father's side told me I should write a book and I wanted to wait until I retired. But I had so much spare time in the pandemic, it was a kind of forced retirement, and a good time to sum up my two decades in the business. I have been a reporter with Bloomberg News and Market News International over this time, and this book follows my experience with the Bank of Canada.

I am a newswire reporter, and used to filing on deadlines of minutes or seconds; I'm not a regular book writer. I don't claim the precision of an academic or the inside knowledge of those who created economic policy over this time. (And if you're fan of footnotes, you will be disappointed.) Hopefully this work will capture the flavour of policy choices that help people in the future.

What is the Bank of Canada and why is it important?

The Bank of Canada's powers go beyond just setting interest rates to control the economy. It also prints bank notes, runs government bond auctions, seeks to control counterfeiting, and oversees some of the financial system's plumbing. It may also soon create a digital currency. My main focus is on monetary policy.

The Bank of Canada's headline events are announcements about its trend-setting interest rate, communicated at eight fixed dates a year. The Governor currently also holds a press conference after each decision, or on the day after, to explain the background thinking. The Bank reserves the right to make a snap move in an emergency. These public events have increased focus on the Bank's view of the economy and, in some cases, have put the Governor on a stronger footing than the Finance Minister. (In the past, the key interest rate had different definitions, and in some phases was even allowed to just be the average of bi-weekly treasury bill auctions, rather than a direct policy tool.)

The Bank's goal today is keeping consumer price inflation increasing at two percent, an aim now loosely shared by most major central banks around the world. The record shows that Canada has been better at meeting this goal than most other nations. To allow domestic prices to stay under the Bank's control, Canada's dollar trades freely in global markets.

This idea of building public understanding around why interest rates are being changed is a big shift from past thinking—that the Bank of Canada didn't need to announce much of anything, much less explain. Governors in decades past could give just a handful of speeches a year, in an era where interest rates were set in the free market, while the dollar was kept fixed under a global system. Today, it's hard to imagine how many more worthwhile events and reports they could put out.

The Bank of Canada, born in the crisis of the Great Depression in 1935, has arguably lurched from one policy focus to another over time, whether it be an inflation target, a fixed currency, or seeking just to end the fear of the Depression. No matter how sound a policy seems, you must always be willing to toss it out in a crisis, or when something better comes along. That's no guarantee that anyone will know when that time for change is, or if the solution will be any better, last any longer, or prevent the next crisis.

What is monetary policy?

My high school economics teacher, Mr. Gillis, called money man's greatest invention and greatest illusion. My journalism ethics teacher argued that the Sabbath, a day of rest in a world awash with capitalism, was the greatest invention. No matter what you think, civilizations need some kind of system to help figure out what to produce, how to produce it, and who gets the rewards of our labour.

The illusion part of money is that the whole financial system would fall apart if people lost faith in money. Dollar bills are just colorful objects, like marbles.

Yet we rarely think about where money comes from or why we use it.

So why do the government and the Bank of Canada employ hundreds of people to prop up the monetary system?

Money has several key attributes. It's universally accepted, it's portable, and it can come in large or small units. This is much better for accounting than, say, a barter system in which you lug your goods to market and swap fish for deer. It allows people to buy and save at little cost. Think of the inconvenience of buying U.S. dollars for a holiday—during which you expect to need cash for tips and small purchases—and imagine doing that on a daily basis.

This system only works if everyone values money and believes the value will last. In primitive days, you could enforce contracts with a club, at best, and you were vulnerable with early money to forgery. When money was issued by private banks, clients were vulnerable to a bank collapse. Yet today we don't blink at five-year car leases, twenty-year mortgages, and governments borrow money for thirty years at a time. (And lately, the Canadian government has borrowed for fifty years.)

Even the modern Canadian dollar is a fairly young invention. Coming into the twentieth century, Canada and the U.S. had great distrust in a government-owned central bank, which could perhaps get caught up in exploiting farmers or concentrating financial power in Toronto, Montreal, or New York. Only the Great Depression created the emergency needed in 1934-35 for Canada to transition to a central bank, and then only after an awkward phase of privately held shares (which are now held by the Finance Minister).

What the central bank does today is provide a government-backed guarantee that money can be used to settle almost all transactions. We now take this for granted, but imagine a world where your no-good cousin gave you a hundred-dollar bill and you didn't know whether to accept it. This is important to think about if Facebook or another crypto giant advances its own form of digital currency.

The trust-in-money issue taken care of, the main job of monetary policy has been to stabilize the economy's performance, either through keeping an eye on the banking system or by seeking to control employment and inflation through interest rates and the supply of money in the economy.

For quite a while, measuring the money supply was seen as the way to avoid rapid inflation. It made sense for a long time; if you suddenly doubled the amount of cash we all had in our bank accounts, we might spend more and send prices surging, while doing little to increase production. This process could wipe out people living on fixed incomes and workers whose wages don't keep up with rising prices.

Today, with so much more money in digital accounts than cash, a trend that predates the internet, the supply of money is no longer such a reliable way to measure the economy's temperature.

The Bank of Canada's standard tool now is the overnight interest rate set on loans between commercial banks, sort of a valve channeling money between savings and investment. If interest rates are low, people will take out mortgages, companies will borrow money to buy new equipment, and the government may run higher deficits because they see them as affordable. When interest rates are high, people tend to save money, taking out a mortgage is dearer, and companies and government cut back on borrowing and spending. The swings between investment and savings are often a big factor in the economic cycle between fast and slow economic growth, or in boom times and recessions.

Interest rates, then, are little more than "the cost of money." If I save money, how much to I get in return? If I borrow money, how much does it cost me? Every dollar in your wallet then "costs" you something, because if you had saved it, you would get some interest for it. With checking account rates often low and fixed, most individuals don't think of this. But if you won the lottery, you would have to think about paying down debt, spending, or finding a place to park the money and make some return on it.

But it's not like today's Governor, Tiff Macklem, comes to your door and rifles through your wallet to remove that twenty bucks you shouldn't be spending on another bag of Cheetos, or tells the banks what to charge on a mortgage. He certainly doesn't leave any cash under your doormat to get you to buy more Christmas presents, either.

So how else does the Bank of Canada regulate the flow of money and the cost of borrowing?

The Bank of Canada has the special power to create money in Canada, influencing the interest rates in the marketplace. It also has a heavy influence on the key rate for overnight loans between big banks, created so that each one can meet legal requirements to balance their books each night. Think of the scene in the movie, *It's a Wonderful Life*, in which the bank inspector shows up and demands to see that the bank is solvent.

As you can imagine, a private bank that doesn't balance its books is in big trouble. But of course, it can take time for some financial transactions to fully clear, so on any given day, they can have extra cash or be short. This system allows them to access a market to get the cash to settle their books, with a little interest. These kinds of rates are guided by the Bank of Canada.

The cost of these overnight loans—about the safest loan anyone could ever make—is a benchmark for the rates on short term corporate and government debt, onward to government bond rates, and then to the rates on corporate bonds. That can influence the stock market as well, because if I can make five percent on a one-year government bond with essentially no risk, I have to make a good deal more in the stock market that year to beat that return and justify the extra risk. The rate that big banks must pay to borrow money is also a big factor in determining the rate you and I get on a mortgage. Banks must pay that interest cost and then decide what to charge you, the same way a corner store would add a markup to the price of a candy bar.

The Bank of Canada's powerful impact on short-term loans is immediate and in lockstep, but its power over these other kinds of lending can fade. That's an important idea known as the "transmission mechanism," which is much like the idea that your car doesn't instantly, or perfectly, pick up speed when you hit the gas pedal. The relative loss of power can be related to the credibility of the Bank of Canada, quirks in the financial system, or simply because the cost of a thirty-year mortgage depends on many other things besides overnight interest rates.

Think of this as the Bank of Canada holding the bottom of a ladder, with the ladder stretched out and tilted upwards. In normal times, investors demand more interest to lend out money for a longer time, so if a two-year bond has a rate of 1.1 percent, a five-year rate might be 1.5 percent, and a thirty-year, 2.8 percent. Think of those loan durations as steps along the ladder the Bank of Canada is holding, and the interest rates as the tilt on the ladder. In most cases, the Bank can raise or lower the whole ladder smoothly, which helps make sure the economy gets the right signal. In the case of trouble, the bank moves the bottom of the ladder but the rest of it wobbles and doesn't move smoothly. In times of big trouble, the Bank could move interest rates and the rest of the ladder doesn't move at all, or moves up when the Bank moves down. This is a very rare situation.

Ultimately, in a free market, investors don't have to listen to the central bank at all, so the smooth transmission of monetary policy isn't a given. But in normal times, major investors are listening carefully. The Bank has more economists than most investment houses do, so its messages about where the economy is heading are credible. Beyond that, policy makers have the power to create money or take it out of the economy. "Don't fight the Fed" is a common bond market expression, meaning that investors can only hold out against the central bank's influence for so long. In 2020, during the Covid pandemic, for example, the Bank started buying federal government bonds to flush the economy with cash and support demand, and within months some investors were complaining that the Bank of Canada was on its way to owning half the market, impeding private pricing of assets. That's power. How much power? The Bank of Canada's balance sheet swelled to 575 billion dollars from 125 billion dollars within a few months. To put that into perspective, the government replaced its entire fleet of fighter jets for a fraction of that money, and a decision that took many years for the government rather than a few months for the Bank.

Most of us live our lives knowing nothing of these operations in debt markets. But it's important to know that, while news reports are dominated by the stock market, in many nations, the bond market is much larger. The stock market can also be strongly influenced by the bond market because the return an investor can get on a safe government bond has a big influence on how much to pay for a riskier stock. So when interest rates on bonds climb, stocks often become less attractive. Finally, while a company can often withstand a slump in its stock price, missing any kind of debt payment is a massive problem.

Given that economic growth is seen as sustainable at about two percent a year, the kind of fine tuning you need from monetary policy to keep things on track can be a big deal.

You can also see the Bank of Canada's actions in the Canadian dollar's exchange rate. Global investors often buy or sell the Canadian dollar based on whether they can park money in our interest-beating debt at a profit over bonds sold in U.S. dollars, Japanese yen, or the euro. Those flows are sometimes so intense that the Bank of Canada only needs to push rates up or down once or twice and the swing in the exchange rate will do a great deal of the work to shift momentum in our economy.

An interest rate increase that strengthens Canada's dollar makes our goods more expensive in the U.S. and abroad. That can depress orders and slow down our economy, like fewer sales of Saskatchewan potash to India or Nova Scotia lobster to Manhattan bistros.

Remember, a slower economy is a good idea if it means keeping inflation from getting out of hand. That prevents people from seeing their groceries cost a lot more, getting you into more arguments with your boss about the cost of living, and making companies less certain about what prices to charge and how much to produce. Even more dangerous than a short-term swing in prices is a self-fulfilling prophecy where people expect ever higher prices, a psychology that's difficult to break. This is especially dangerous when rising prices for goods and services last long enough for people to demand higher annual pay increases, known as a "wage-price spiral."

Since the 1990s, the Bank of Canada has set an agreement with the government on its main policy goal, and for quite a while, this has been to keep the annual rate of consumer price inflation at two percent. (Consumer price inflation, really the Consumer Price Index, is the cost of a huge group of goods and services that should reflect what families buy each month, from butter to internet hookup, all given a certain share in a bigger index. While there are some complaints that the CPI doesn't effectively capture the cost of living for some families, it's a figure used across the world and a credible alternative has never taken hold.)

There has also been a long debate over whether there is any real magic to an inflation target of two percent, in practice it's turned out to be a sweet spot in Canada, and across most other developed nations, too. Inflation at this pace is slow enough that people don't worry their life savings will be eroded away by higher prices. It is enough to make sure that workers still see their paychecks rising every year, and for firms to pay more to their suppliers. While economists think that stable prices in theory should mean prices should really have an inflation rate close to zero, actual humans don't want to live in a world where one year their wages rise, most years they are unchanged, and sometimes they will take a pay cut.

If that all sounds boring, let's make it more concrete. Everything we pay for is in Canadian dollars. If inflation suddenly perks up, companies must decide if they can raise prices even faster, and workers will ask for higher wage increases. Investors in government and corporate bonds will also demand a higher rate of interest to make sure that when they are repaid their money, they will get a fair return, given that things will cost that much more. If faster inflation gets really fast, everyone will ask for more and more to get ahead of the trend of rising prices. This can reach a point where our daily lives aren't dominated by doing good work or investing in the right projects, but how to get more dollars in your pocket to cover rising prices. This is no longer an economy; it's a lottery.

This kind of instability is one big reason why Canada needed a central bank, and there was resistance to this idea until the Great Depression in the 1930s. Before then, most experts believed in the free market and that "laissez-faire" policies would eventually correct any problems. But back then, the problem was the cycle running in reverse, with prices falling again and again, and this "deflation" leading to a dangerous cycle in which those with money realized that every month they waited, prices for new stoves and cars would be lower. This was a major part of the mass unemployment and distress of the era beyond the famous stock market crash.

Clearly, we haven't had a deflationary spiral recently, even amid the 2020 recession. In fact, broad inflation hardly ever turned negative during this difficult time.

One reason for that, besides massive fiscal relief, was that after the Bank of Canada cut interest rates to about zero in March of 2020, it started shoveling money onto the balance sheets of the big commercial banks, buying up some of their assets, and basically leaving them with a pile of safe cash. (Well, not physical cash, but you get the idea.) This was known as "quantitative easing" (QE), something we avoided in 2008, but would deploy during the Covid pandemic.

But where does that money come from? Good question. At some level, the Bank of Canada simply buys up government bonds and creates money out of thin air to pay for them. The liability of the cash the Bank of Canada has created is balanced out by the asset of the debt they have purchased, and the borrower now must pay back to the central bank. In reverse, the Bank of Canada can sell assets off its balance sheet into financial markets, take the cash away and make it disappear if that's needed to slow the economy.

Put another way, the central bank is a bank for commercial banks. The Bank of Canada doesn't just put stacks of twenties into Brinks trucks and ship them to Toronto, it also oversees key payment systems and works with international regulators on best practices. In a crisis, the Bank of Canada can help mediate market panic—that's a valuable intangible.

The Bank of Canada is also the government's banker, arranging bond auctions, doing consultations with markets, and advising the Finance Minister on economic developments. This is a helpful outside voice for a government to have.

As I write this, I am reminded that in my economics schooling, textbooks devoted thousands of pages to theories of how firms behaved, or microeconomics, and how national economies acted, macroeconomics, and reams of statistical tools for measuring all of both. There were a few pages at the back of the books about monetary policy, and even fewer on unconventional tools.

Halfway through the 2008 bank collapse, I went back and checked this. It was clear that for most of us, probably even the experts were writing new history. The lesson is that a crisis is something for which you often have little preparation, no matter how prepared you think you are.

At that point, you must use your experience and guts to feel your way around. As journalists, we lived under the strain of the deep unknown for more than a year, even in stable Canada. When I saw experts starting to throw around terms like quantitative easing and conditional commitments, I knew there was no very deep well for them to draw from. And market investors who leaned on them as precise terms often could not come up with a satisfying answer when pressed about what exactly the parameters of these terms were. They were what was spelled out for us at the time, subject to revisions later.

To return to where I started, the idea of money itself, now we stand at a time when private digital money may soon compete with the currency controlled by the central banks.

One thing my time in Ottawa has shown me is that the ultimate question of whether something should be private or public is who is responsible when it collapses? If it's something that can survive a corporate bankruptcy, you could argue it can be private. If it's something with a larger human cost, or an important service that can't survive a corporate bankruptcy, or even the physical destruction of a headquarters, then government probably needs at least a stake in the thing. We saw this realignment after 9/11 as the government laid out legislation on conditions for nationalizing international bridges, which are important, but for most of history were seen as important but something that a firm could build, have destroyed, a rebuild as needed.

When it comes to money, which depends heavily on the public perception that it is an eternal store of value, I gravely doubt it can be put into private hands again. I don't want my life savings in a currency that isn't backed by a government. (People living in countries with very high inflation will have a different view of this.) One of the most basic reforms of the Great Depression was deposit insurance, so that even if your bank collapses, the government will make good on your basic savings. Facebook or other digital currencies can't really give me that guarantee.

In modern times, as we think of whether Mark Zuckerberg can create a world digital currency, or whether Apple can, ask yourself if any corporation can really underpin a currency. While managing digital transfers of money is one thing, protecting the actual wealth and value of money is something else. Yet online commentators seem to have taken the discussion in the opposite direction, suggesting it's safer to avoid government-controlled money.

For Canada, competing currencies, controlled perhaps by U.S. firms, and not denominated in Canadian dollars, could damage our independent monetary policy. So rather than a professional effort to control inflation and the turns from boom to bust in the economy, the supply of money would be dictated by forces we don't understand. The Bank of Canada also makes a form of profit know as seigniorage from the interest-bearing assets it buys when it sends money out into the world, giving most of it to the federal government. Does a private company deserve to potentially skim that profit for itself for a system that is fundamentally for Canadians?

Having said all this, it's important to remember that today's central banking regime is the result of trial and error, setbacks, and the economy's changing needs. Luckily, historians point out that the preamble to the Bank of Canada Act gives very wide latitude.

Read it over several times, it's that broad:

WHEREAS it is desirable to establish a central bank in Canada to regulate credit and currency in the best interests of the economic life of the nation, to control and protect the external value of the national monetary unit and to mitigate by its influence fluctuations in the general level of production, trade, prices and employment, so far as may be possible within the scope of monetary action, and generally to promote the economic and financial welfare of Canada […]

When we look at any current discussion of whether the Bank can or should enact any specific emergency policy, recall how wide-ranging Parliament's original orders were.

In the early days, the tools included "moral suasion," the idea of calling up banks and suggesting they do this or that. The financial system back then seemed small and simple enough for a few friendly or unfriendly phone calls to smooth things out.

Through the 1930s, World War II, and beyond, there was also a lot of work managing things such as fixed exchange rates, and destabilizing swings in our international balance of payments. This required a lot of technical maneuvering. Canada was a bit of a rebel by busting out of the fixed exchange-rate system known as Bretton Woods (created around the end of World War Two). With our small and trade-reliant economy, we were really an early warning system, showing how this global order would fail.

Later, the supply of money was seen as key to managing the economy, and especially keeping governments from dangerous inflation bred by lax fiscal policy. This "monetarist" thinking, led by Milton Friedman, was the antidote to politicians using Keynesian economics to justify ever-expanding government and deficits. John Maynard Keynes in fact advocated a balanced approach to government fiscal policy, with surpluses in good times to balance the deficits in bad times, but politicians often have other ideas.

Focus on the money supply started breaking down over time, because of changes in the nature of savings and checking accounts and in the banking system discussed earlier. (Children often laugh when I tell them this story from the 1980s about banking, illustrating how much ideas of "money supply" and the economy have changed: My Dad used to take us to the mall on Friday nights to cash his paycheque, take out some money from a teller, and go buy groceries.)

Some Bank of Canada officials became fond of saying they didn't give up on the of money supply, but rather that the money supply gave up on them.

The idea of instead using interest rates to target a rate of inflation came first in New Zealand, and then in Canada in the early 1990s. This came about in Canada mostly out of government fear that the new Goods and Services Tax (GST) would spark a rush of inflation that would get out of hand. (I recall that, at the time, concern about inflation was justified by a campaign of retailers putting "Don't Blame Me for the GST" stickers on cash registers.) Generally, it was a miserable time for Canada, and the GST was part of a bigger dose of bitter medicine as the economy also went through a difficult recession. Governments had to rein in spending and deficits as it was becoming very difficult to sell new bonds, especially to foreign investors.

The inflation targeting system worked. The numerical target for inflation was kept in place after the initial success, and for a long time the target itself has remained at two percent. (The first target was higher at three percent and it was lowered as inflation came down.)

This is still no easy job, mostly because after you raise or lower interest rates, just about the last impact of the change is on inflation. Even the Bank says it can take two years for the full impact of its moves to be felt on the inflation rate. (Most of the impact is felt in the first year though.) One big reason for that is annual wage contracts. If you seek to slow the economy in January, some people may have just negotiated their pay for the next year, and there's no chance to adjust the pace of pay raises for another year. The impact of that faster or slower growth in incomes and spending doesn't show up until the end of the year after that.

In other words, if you want to stop inflation getting out of control, you may have to see it coming up to two years in advance. Another risk: if you see inflation rocketing up today and you raise interest rates, by the time that feeds into the economy, it may have gone into a slump and you have injected exactly the wrong medicine.

This is why central bankers lard their speeches with endless references to uncertainty and thinking about the future. It's not easy to figure out if what you are doing today will be the right thing when the bulk of the impact is a year away, but policy decisions must still be taken in the here-and-now. In many cases, by the time you see inflation getting off track, if you haven't already acted on it, you're too late.

Canada's dollar is another wild card. Global investors sometimes buy and sell our currency on the strength of our economy or moves from our central bank, which is helpful. Other times, global investors buy and sell our currency because of wider global trends that are at odds with the direction our economy needs to go, which makes it harder for our economy to go in the right direction.

And traders in New York, Tokyo, or London can switch their positions very quickly from bullish to bearish, making the currency a problem in a hurry.

Governors must also explain all of this in English and French, and appear several times a year before parliamentary committees, where lawmakers can grill them about any piece of this system. What's more likely is that lawmakers spend two hours trying to trick central bankers into providing a quote they can twist into an endorsement of their party's economic platform.

While Governors may dread the political pitfalls of testifying at parliamentary committees, lawmakers have mostly kept the central bank's day-to-day operations at arms length—with good reason. There can be temptation during election season to boost the economy just in time for the vote.

Parliament can certainly rush through big and irresponsible spending measures to boost their election fortunes, but even a majority government can't easily force monetary policy to play along. Voters can also observe any implicit clashes on economic policy between a big-spending government and a central bank responding with higher interest rates to keep the economy from overheating.

Imagine, for example, a world in which the Finance Minister can lower mortgage rates at will. Given the cycle of spending that would set off over the next two years, it could be destructive. And would a government ever have the will needed to drive up interest rates as inflation took hold, or to resist cutting rates at the slightest sign of economic weakness?

As long as Kings and Queens have put their faces on gold coins, the risk of a government debasing its own currency has often been great.

What's in it for me, or
How the Bank of Canada affects your trip to Florida, your mortgage, the price of gas at the pumps, and the cost of the government's deficit

Here are the questions I am asked most often.

Should I take a fixed or variable rate mortgage?

The most frequent question I have been asked over time is by someone who has a mortgage that's coming up for renewal—either a fixed-rate or a floating rate loan. They wonder what the best option is. With the recent jump in interest rates, the answer is more difficult. In the years before Covid, when interest rates were very low, my thought was that if the question was about locking in for rates that were historically low but could go even lower, it seemed more comfortable to lock in to guard against the risk that rates would rise. There seemed little benefit in trying to see rates go continually lower, and the flip side, of course, is illustrated by the pain people are seeing now from the rate surge.

An older generation reminds us that in the high inflation times of the 1970s and 80s, mortgage rates were often around twenty percent! There's little evidence today that we are returning to anywhere near those rates. There's also little evidence we will return to the record low borrowing costs on a sustained basis.

I'm not a personal financial planner, but the main consideration to me is what will keep you up at night. If you aren't comfortable with worrying about rates moving around, lock in for a five-year term. The bigger issue I have is that people aren't saving up twenty percent or more for a down payment, the cut-off line for federal mortgage insurance. My paternal grandparents lived through the Great Depression, and I saw that, for the rest of their lives, they had a visceral dislike of debt, and were very proud to say they had saved and paid off their mortgage and car loans as soon as they could.

Is this a good time to buy U.S. dollars for my vacation?

Investors sometimes say the Canadian dollar suffers from a "random walk." That is, there's no one factor that drives the exchange rate, so betting on it going up or down is tough even for the experts. The best bet is to assume that today's exchange rate will be the same as tomorrow's. So again, if it makes you feel safer to buy months in advance, or you feel safer buying just before your travel, you are correct. The only thing I have noticed is that there are often big gaps between retail and professional prices for U.S. dollars, so shopping around is wise. And watch out for extra fees at airport terminals and ATMs. Finally, if there isn't an explicit transaction fee, remember that cost is just is being shoved into the quoted exchange rate.

Is this a good time to buy U.S. dollars for my vacation? Again, the answer to that question is really whatever helps you sleep at night. The dollar can move on so many variables, it's actually better to focus on finding a vendor who doesn't add a big chunk of fees, hidden or otherwise.

And if you think you can day-trade the dollar, consider how much the pros are doing to beat you. As an example, a friend of mine who ended up working on Wall Street told me over a swanky steak dinner that he downloaded spreadsheets every night to track each trade in a certain type of security I had never even heard of. He looked for inconsistencies and patterns to make other profitable trades.

Subscribers to financial news services also pay big money to see market-moving headlines exactly when they are released, and trade accordingly. Financial newswires time headlines and releases of market-moving economics statistics to fractions of a second. We get figures such as the unemployment rate for release at 8:30 a.m. from Statistics Canada in Ottawa, but we also get an hour of time to read the reports and prepare well-organized stories and headlines. Reporters are locked in a room with no ability to transmit anything until the right time.

So when the unemployment rate is published out at what you and I would call 8:30 a.m., in fact to the wires, it would be more like 8:30:00. Try beating that with your internet account, which is probably slower than what the major trading houses have paid for.

Where are gasoline prices going?

On gasoline prices, you're on your own. It's a complicated line from global crude oil prices to refining costs to what the large retail gasoline station chains do with prices. You could really ask the question that "muckraker" journalist Ida Tarbell posed long ago: how has a commodity that, at the beginning, anyone could grab out of the ground, become such a monopolistic industry? In other words, oil doesn't strictly trade on market forces.

These questions, which I get quite often, point to something important in economics and central banking. Most people tend to focus on a few narrow items in forming their views of prices and the economy. Mortgage and housing costs, the price of gas to fill up the car, and sometimes the Canadian dollar and the cost of sunny vacations.

While economists know that the monthly inflation reports give a pretty good picture of the overall cost of living, the perceptions of real people are often quite different. The Bank of Canada's own consumer expectations survey showed a very dubious trend of people expecting much higher inflation over a long period of time than any economist would accept. Governor Tiff Macklem has spoken during the pandemic about how inflation feels higher during the pandemic than the official figures show. And while Statistics Canada readjusted the consumer price index to better reflect that fact that people replaced restaurant meals with groceries, and trips to Florida or movie theaters with a Netflix subscription, the overall difference wasn't that large.

While economists are always seeking to improve mapping human behaviour onto how they map out the economy, it's tough. Tracking dollars is a clear way of measuring things, but expectations and motivations are important and much harder to get at. Our "lizard brains" are swayed when we see gasoline prices posted every time we drive, and pay them every week when we fill up the car. If a liter of gas moves from ninety-five cents to $1.25, we notice.

What we don't seem to notice is items that have gone down significantly. When I was a kid, my parents paid 600 or 800 dollars to buy a Beta VCR and were thrilled to have one. About a decade ago, in a back aisle of Walmart, we paid a hundred fifty dollars for a VCR and DVD player, and we weren't sure we would be using it even a few years later. Today you can go to Value Village and buy a used DVD player for next to nothing. As for a television, I had a black-and-white TV in my bedroom when I was a kid and was considered lucky. Today we have a flat screen that's twice as large, and recently, a ten-year-old boy came to our house and laughed at us for having such a small TV. We surely paid, after adjusting for inflation, far less for this marvel than my parents did for the two-color TV I had back then. (Also, the importance of a

TV has declined substantially with people streaming videos on their phones and tablets.)

Since we only buy a TV occasionally, and because so many new products are coming along, we just don't remember how much we save on these items. On the flip side, most of our utility bills quietly creep up year after year and keep a constant hold over a good chunk of our budget. Yet how many of us are willing to call up the insurance or phone company every couple of years to get the best price? There's clearly something going on with our sensitivity to the changes in the prices of some products over others, and that's just one way inflation is hard to predict.

Some economists build their models of consumer spending based on the idea that people are very rational, taking in all the price changes and the Bank of Canada's goal of keeping inflation at two percent, and behaving accordingly. Others see that consumers are more likely to just react to price changes after the fact.

The way Canadians respond to changes in inflation underlines the challenging gap between what experts use to measure the economy and what people end up doing with their money. This is probably why the Bank of Canada has given hundreds of speeches in every nook and cranny of Canada, touting its goals, to bridge that gap in understanding. It could be a problem of the Bank speaking in language the public doesn't understand, or it could be that the economic profession fails to capture human motivations when it calculates inflation and GDP. That said, it's unfair to hold economists to the same standards as physicists—while the movement of the planets is fairly constant, the behaviour of people and the products they buy keeps changing.

One final example of this is while the overall inflation rate is useful, for any individual the cost of living can be different. Seniors don't buy school supplies, downtown condo dwellers often don't buy as much gas, low-income families aren't worried about the cost of a flight to Florida.

Why doesn't the Bank of Canada just follow U.S. monetary policy?

Another frequent question I hear, and it's a fair one, is why doesn't Canada follow the latest U.S. move on interest rates by the Federal Reserve? If they cut, why didn't we cut? If their rate is higher or lower than ours, why didn't we just match it? Bank of Canada Governors always seemed to struggle with this question, not just from journalists but from public audiences as well. I never heard the perfect answer, so here's mine. Think of our economies as the front lawns of my house and your house. If my wife says she saw the neighbours cut their grass yesterday, the implication is, when am I going to cut our grass? While we both have the same kind of grass and the same weather, our lawns may still have different needs because I may use fertilizer at different times, I may have a tree that gives a different amount of shade to the yard, or we may water the grass differently. (Yes, I could also be lazy or inattentive.) While it makes no sense to ignore what my neighbour is doing, it could also be unwise to cut the grass just because my neighbour did.

Having mentioned that questions come to Governors from the public after speeches as well as from us "pros" in the media, I will admit this. Governors often made a special effort to answer questions from the public after speeches. And those questions often got to an obvious point we had missed. I've learned to appreciate it.

When it comes to whether it's a good time to lock in a mortgage or buy U.S. dollars, from what I've seen, the difficulty is this: currencies, especially, can rise or fall on just about any kind of information because they are traded to pay for any kind of good or service across nations. Canada's dollar can move against the U.S. dollar based on anything that happens here, or on anything that happens in the U.S.

Because the U.S. dollar is the world's "reserve currency;" that is, it's used as a default for companies and people who want a reliable store of purchasing power, the U.S. dollar is also prone to move on any global trend. People often buy and sell U.S. dollars simply because they think, for example, that the U.K. economy is more-or-less secure because of Brexit, that Japan is either going to get out of its long-term funk or not, or because Russia will do well or poorly with shifting oil prices. And, in the short term, currencies don't even move on economic fundamentals like GDP, interest rates, or inflation. They can also move on political risk, and simply because there are large investors out there who are speculating on it going one way or the other. There are also pros who trade in currencies based on "technical" factors, which again, is hard to figure out, but essentially, they look at historical trading for predictable patterns to profit from, patterns in reports about overall trading positions, and whether people have taken out a lot of contracts to buy or sell currencies. Others also have pre-set orders to buy or sell under certain conditions, meaning that sometimes, if pre-programmed orders line up wrong, the currency can suddenly spike or fall if the bets are all triggered at the same time. So if you can give me the entire state of every other financial market, plus political developments, I would still have a very imperfect chance of telling you where the U.S. or Canadian dollar will trade a month from today.

CHAPTER TWO

Finding What Works from What Failed

What has the current system gotten right?

By the standards of central banking, today's system has been in place for a long time. It has helped pull Canada through some very tough challenges, and policy makers have also made wise and timely changes to make it even more fit for the job at hand today.

The current inflation target is reviewed every five years, and most reviews have largely rubber-stamped the system. This process of review is something of a strength in itself, preventing the bureaucratic forces of inertia from becoming too strong. The Federal Reserve has recently emulated some of the system.

The regular reviews also help with democratic accountability, giving the government a voice and sharing the blame if things go wrong. No government should accuse the Bank of Canada of pursuing a dangerous goal when it shares in the creation of the mission statement. Most Finance Ministers are careful in affirming the Bank of Canada's independence. This is a good thing in a world where many countries often see central bank independence as a convenience granted by political leaders rather than something that benefits the public and the economy. Look at places like Russia, Turkey, Latin America and even the potentially fire-able Federal Reserve Chair under U.S. President Donald Trump.

The Bank of Canada spends quite a lot of time in each five-year cycle looking at how it could improve, which in some ways takes away from other work it could be doing, and sometimes has the hallmark of a PR campaign rather than a providing a genuine sense that change is coming. Given the success of inflation targeting, it would perhaps be wise to extend the review term to something like eight or ten years. If a government elected to a traditional four-year term isn't guaranteed the chance to formally adjust the central bank's mandate in the regular review that comes every five years, why should an un-elected Governor with a seven-year term be guaranteed a chance to tinker with it? The system is also now three decades old and has largely stood the test of time, so maybe an eight or nine-year cycle is sufficient.

The public often sees journalists as cynical. So, as an antidote, here is some more specific credit where it's due on the Bank.

Increased transparency

Governors John Crow, Gordon Thiessen, and David Dodge moved to boost transparency in a way that has been under-appreciated. Stephen Poloz also did a fine job seeking to simplify some overly complicated points around the Bank's economic forecasts and speak more plainly to the public. All this dovetailed with the digital media era and the more recent move to global populism, where increasing the distance, metaphorically speaking, from the public would have been even more dangerous. There are now more speeches, more details around the Bank's economic projections, and more press conferences than when I began covering the Bank twenty years ago. Again, some of these practices have been followed by the Fed in the U.S., with the Chair holding regular press conferences after rate decisions.

Bringing down inflation

Canada's painful fight to bring down inflation in the early 1990s was largely done under Governor John Crow. I never covered him as Governor, but I interviewed him after he published his memoir. While he might have liked to have a second term to enjoy the fruits of his labour, his willingness to bring inflation down with tighter policy laid the foundation for much of what we have now. The price he paid was taking some of the blame for the tough 1990-91 recession. The government at the time was also seemingly fearful that the hated GST would add to the economy's burdens to drive inflation up—another example of how crisis helps revamp policy. Since Governor Crow took on that crisis, there was quite a long period during which the Bank was free from the tough job of breaking an era of stubborn high inflation. While inflation reached about eight percent in 2022, the benefits of the past fight are still paying off. Even the most aggressive forecasts see the Bank of Canada's interest rates holding below five percent. Compare that with previous generations who took out mortgages at rates well over ten percent.

Meeting the two percent target

Until recently, the Bank of Canada has had great success in meeting its target of inflation at two percent, more success than its peers at the Bank of Japan, the U.S. Federal Reserve, and the European Central Bank have seen. That's about three decades of good performance.

The resilience of this goal speaks to how well it has worked. One main argument, especially at the start of inflation targeting, was whether setting inflation at two percent was too high a target. Why not set it lower and really let people know you mean business about keeping the cost of living in check? The main consideration I have seen from experts is the idea that, while people may indeed enjoy a world where prices don't rise too fast, there could be a problem on the wage side if there are frequently years in which salaries are stagnant.

Of course, the dangers of extreme inflation are something we forgot about until just recently, coming out of the Covid pandemic. But over history, countries that lose control of inflation have big problems with social stability. Germany, in particular, has always been seen as favouring tight monetary policy and tough inflation control because of its experience after World War

I with what's called hyperinflation. More recently, Zimbabwe and Venezuela have had this problem.

Avoiding the use of emergency tools

In my opinion, the experiences of the Federal Reserve, Bank of Japan and European Central Bank suggest it's much harder to get out of emergency policies than they would like to admit. To my mind, the Bank of Canada resisted going all in amid the 2008 and 2020 recessions, giving itself more room to raise rates later. More importantly, it didn't have to use the lender of last resort powers as much, which I think is a good thing. Even today, it seems clear that the Bank of Canada's asset purchases are something that policy makers are moving to scale back as soon as the market can handle them again. This also helps avoid the perception that investors or the government have "captured" the central bank or roped it into a bailout. Also, when financial markets or even the housing market, crashes, perhaps governments, rather than central banks, should be the main clean-up crew, given that that work must involve difficult political choices around choosing who is saved. Minneapolis Fed President Neel Kashkari, who helped design the U.S. bailout policies around the 2008 crisis, has said in that, in hindsight, very few homeowners found relief, while the banks were saved.

Setting a wide range around the target

The target is two percent and that's what we hear most often, but they have a band around it that's quite wide, one percent to three percent. And they give themselves two years to bring inflation back to target. Those objectives aren't without detractors, who say that so much wiggle room isn't really price stability at all. By setting a wide band around the two percent inflation target, the Canada gives itself a lot of room to overlook short term trends. Other central banks have stumbled around the idea that the two percent goal, when they set it, was really a ceiling and policy makers cared more about keeping inflation below two percent than above it. This wider range in Canada is also beneficial because it avoids letting people think you can ever really be that precise in the short-term, or even the medium term. Central banks can't ever target inflation down to exactly 2.0 percent all the time. The best they can generally do is keep it somewhere around there, some of the time.

Learning from past failures, and Parliamentary oversight

The Bank recognizes that the way it operates today is by no means a guarantee of future success. The path to how it operates today was long and complicated by various failures: trying to control the exchange rate, until even changing interest rates failed to stop eager traders; the abandonment of the worship of the money supply as the way to control the economy; a global system of fixed exchange rates that we slipped out of, to the chagrin of the International Monetary Fund (IMF), before the rest of the world caught on to the flaws of the Bretton Woods system (adopted in 1944).

Beyond the wide-ranging preamble of the Bank of Canada Act the rest of the legislation does have some interesting consequences on how it acts:

First, the Bank of Canada is clearly established as a creature of Parliament. When some complain about a rogue central bank or priests in a temple, remember that the government always holds final control, just as it does with the military or other institutions of state. There was a painful incident with former Governor James Coyne, during which it became clear that the legislation had no clear way of resolving a major dispute on policy direction. After that situation, it's understood that the recourse for a government that feels monetary policy is wrecking Canada is to have the Finance Minister deliver a message to Parliament that the government has an issue. Governors faced with this message are generally expected to resign. This is a very helpful nuclear option, one that prevents a government from attempting to manage day to day Bank of Canada affairs. It also makes clear to the Bank that the government can launch that missile.

For more details, this is what the Bank of Canada Act says about the power to direct the central bank:

Government Directive

Consultations

14 (1) The Minister and the Governor shall consult regularly on monetary policy and on its relation to general economic policy.

(2) If, notwithstanding the consultations provided for in subsection (1), there should emerge a difference of opinion between the Minister and the Bank concerning the monetary policy to be followed, the Minister may, after consultation with the Governor and with the approval of the Governor in Council, give to the Governor a written directive concerning monetary policy, in specific terms and applicable for a specified period, and the Bank shall comply with that directive.

Publication and report

(3) A directive given under this section shall be published forthwith in the *Canada Gazette* and shall be laid before Parliament within fifteen days after the giving thereof, or, if Parliament is not then sitting, on any of the first fifteen days next thereafter that either House of Parliament is sitting.

The legislation also says that Governors "shall each be appointed for a term of seven years during good behaviour." Lawyers can debate exactly what that means, but to me, it does not sound like a Governor can be dismissed while performing ordinary duties.

Another good check on government interference is the seven-year term mentioned above. That means a government must win two election mandates to guarantee the ability to replace the Governor at the end of a regular term. This helps ward off any perception that any government would put a political litmus test on what is a technocratic job.

The government also doesn't directly appoint the Governor, or the Senior Deputy. There is a board of directors that represents the provinces and the business community that nominates the candidates to the Finance Minister in cabinet. This is another check on political influence.

There is also a back door here. The Finance Minister, over time, names the directors, so over the space of several years, as directors get replaced, you can have a situation where a government can gain influence. It seems fair to believe that a Finance Minister that has a really strong feeling can easily make a phone call to a director to lobby for or against a candidate. there has never been a proven link between partisan considerations and who becomes Governor, and I don't know of any such situation.

Early in my career, the appointment of David Dodge created media shockwaves, because he was Deputy Finance Minister under Paul Martin. At the time there were stories about how the finance department or minister would dominate, but those were put to rest pretty quickly.

That situation did start a trend of passing over the Senior Deputy Governor and finding an outside candidate to lead the central bank. By now, it seems unlikely that any Senior Deputy can now believe they are a lock for the top job. It has been pointed out that this must corrode the internal culture at the Bank to believe you can't work your way from the mail room to the Governor's office. However, at the salary range for the Senior Deputy's slot, I could be snubbed, too. (The salary ranges for the Governor and Senior Deputy in 2017 as listed on the Bank's website are: Governor, 463,100–544,800 dollars; Senior Deputy Governor, 324,300-381,500 dollars.)

Other parts of the Bank of Canada Act lay out a provision I find is often misunderstood, even by journalists who should know better. The act provides for the sensible idea that the Governor and Finance Minister should be in regular contact with each other to discuss policy. After all, do you really want a Governor saying one thing about the economy in a breakfast speech in Montreal and the Finance Minister saying the opposite an hour later in Toronto? More to the point, the Bank of Canada helps oversee some of the plumbing of the banking system, is the banker for the government, runs its bond auctions, and so on. Hard to do that if you aren't talking to your client. The meetings have always been private, of course, but every so often you see stories about a leak from one of the meetings, often with the insinuation that there an emergency or dispute brewing.

The Act also laid down a lot of powers for emergency action, such as buying up securities as the lender of last resort. One wise change was that the government more or less turned this work over to the Bank of Canada. Compare this with 2020 when the Federal Reserve needed Treasury approval for some of its special programs to unclog markets. And by the end of the year, Secretary Mnuchin said that some of these extraordinary powers would expire, prompting the Fed to put out a rare statement suggesting it would have done things differently if it could have. This is not the kind of sniping you want in a crisis. In Europe, the ECB has had some of its emergency measures subject to German court challenges—again, not what you want in a crisis.

In 2020, the Bank of Canada was quickly able to mostly call its own shots and, not only buy up federal government bonds, but provincial bonds, and some corporate bonds as well. You may debate the merits of this, but at least we didn't have many politicians entering the fray about whether we should be backstopping Newfoundland and Alberta bonds, or bonds of companies like Air Canada, for example.

The power in practice: Code words to guide the economy

While moving interest rates up and down is a powerful tool, as are the current bond purchases, it's arguably not the main way the central bank keeps the economy running smoothly.

With its speeches, press conferences and research agenda, the Bank has a big influence on how financial markets and the public see the economy. When Canada's big commercial banks see the Bank of Canada overhaul its forecast, their own economists face some pressure on their own projections. Finance Ministers can also be asked tough questions if there is a big gap between the outlook they are giving versus that of the central bank.

For financial market pros, the numbers are one thing, but it's more often a small number of key phrases that are seen as clues to whether interest rates are on hold or going higher or lower. People who trade the Canadian dollar and bonds make or lose a lot of money in an instant if the market swings for or against them, and a central bank speech is one event that can often set the tone for markets.

While the Bank of Canada is moving to use much more plain language, its statements often contain phrases that investors call "forward guidance" or "policy bias."

Minute changes in expressions like "reducing significant monetary stimulus" to "reducing monetary stimulus" are hounded over by market watchers and journalists. The difference implied by removing the word "significant" is that it implies the Bank is closer to where interest rates need to go. Another recent example is the different between saying interest rates "could rise" and saying such tightening could be "forceful," because the extra word implies the moves could be bigger than the regular quarter of a percentage point. This may sound like over-interpretation, but for a bond or pension fund manager making trades worth millions of dollars on a regular basis, very small deviations in interest rates can be costly. (Even costlier: I did once hear a bond trader ask a trainer what he could do if he accidentally hit "buy" instead of "sell.")

The benefit of these slight word changes is they allow a Governor to hint to financial markets about a course of action without having to make a firm commitment. This allows financial markets to do some of the central bank's work for it in moving interest rates up or down to slow or speed up economic growth. In situations where the economic outlook is unclear, it allows policymakers more flexibility to change course if the economy moves in a different direction.

In the deep recessions around 2008 and 2020, Governors Carney and Macklem also offered up a "conditional commitment," a pledge to hold interest rates until inflation or the broader economy made a big improvement, with some sort of explicit timeframe in mind. This has been helpful in an emergency. It's also led to a lot of debate about whether this creates the danger of later being forced to break a clear promise.

Governors have expressed ambivalence about the demand for such code words, and how investors tend to over interpret one or two sentences and ignore the bigger themes in play. Governors often say their job isn't to hand out breadcrumbs to markets or to make the future path of its actions appear certain or fixed.

There is no perfect answer to the question of whether it's better to avoid these phrases and let the markets figure it out, or whether guidance is always helpful. The job is also complicated by the fact a public official often has an obligation to tamp down fears of worst-case scenarios, which can create a self-fulfilling prophecy.

While Governor Stephen Poloz insisted that he disdained such code words, inevitably he slipped into them a few times. In some ways, it's hard not to talk about future trends that apply to interest rates when you forecast the economy two years out, and your job is to show how you will meet an inflation target.

One clear benefit of giving investors subtle hints is that that it can help improve the transmission of monetary policy into the real economy. One possible definition of bad policy is that every time the Bank changes interest rates by a quarter percentage point, market interest rates move much more or much less. In the worst situation, interest rates move in the opposite direction because the central bank has lost credibility with investors.

The downside is that markets do get addicted to buzzwords. I have seen many private investment houses blindly publish forecasts that just parrot the Bank of Canada's views, even when the Bank's projections show contradictions that are cause for a rethink. Other market economists sometimes put out very confident forecasts, based on the Bank's simplified rhetoric, but casting aside any nuance about the risks of things going off course. Some economics shops come out with clickbait forecasts: "Bank of Canada on hold for three years!"

In summary, the public isn't harmed by code words and markets can benefit when they are used wisely, so that's about as far as I can see the benefits. In a crisis, they can also be a way to build confidence and reduce business uncertainty, but Governors must be careful to make promises they can keep, and be aware that there can be consequences on if promises aren't kept, on them and on future Governors.

Dangers of oversharing

One controversy for media and practitioners is whether the Bank of Canada should become even more candid. The most common option suggested is that the Bank should publish minutes of their meetings, even perhaps the individual votes. The other, more radical, suggestion is that the Bank should publish an interest rate forecast, something Norway does explicitly, or something like the Fed's "dot plot," through which the committee members suggest, anonymously, where they see rates being in the medium term, and at various points before then.

The Bank of Canada has announced that, starting in 2023, it will indeed publish a form of meeting minutes, based on a review of its transparency practices by the International Monetary Fund. Canada indeed has been an outlier in not providing these details. So we will indeed see how much clarity they provide.

I stick with my view Canada's track record speaks for itself, and I don't see how publishing meeting minutes will make the Bank better at doing its job. The Bank has opted not to identify individual comments, so that mitigates a concern about whether policy makers will be distracted when it comes to setting the best policy for the future because they are looking over their shoulders at their own track record.

The big thing people overlook is that the Bank of Canada Act specifies that the Governor alone (and perhaps the Senior Deputy if something happens to the Governor) sets monetary policy. Any published vote showing dissent has no merit in law. And of course, the nightmare scenario would be a Governor accountable to Parliament, but somehow outvoted in an internal Bank meeting. At that point, wouldn't Parliament be bound to consider removing a Governor? In an extreme case, could the deputies stage some kind of coup?

This argument is a bit facetious, but the point is that I don't see the Bank of Canada ever volunteering to go to Parliament to empower deputies, the fear being that opposition parties or the government itself would open the full text of the Bank of Canada Act to impose other unhelpful changes.

We already had one small case of this, an accountability act where Crown corporations must produce quarterly reports just like private companies. The Bank of Canada objected and was turned down. Of course, the Bank of Canada is not a profit-making enterprise, its goals are strictly public policy and supporting the economy.

If you read the quarterly Bank of Canada financial reports, they are absurd. A neat breaking out of profits and revenues, all filled with disclosures about how this isn't the point. I bet no lawmakers read them anyway, nor the public, but it ties up employees and accountants. For those who care, the Bank does submit an annual report to Parliament that is far more germane.

Macklem and Poloz have argued strongly that their expanded opening statements before quarterly press conferences and "report card" speeches after other rate decisions are in fact a form of meeting minutes. (There are eight decisions a year, four with full economic forecasts known as the Monetary Policy Reports, and four without. The Monetary Policy Reports began in 1995 under Gordon Thiessen, and at first, were semi-annual.)

While the idea that these statements are truly meeting minutes is clearly debatable, there's no question that the statements have details that former

Governors did not want to put out in the public domain. We do get a flavour of the discussions we didn't before. And that can be helpful in back-and-forth discussions about cases where they held rates, but could have raised or lowered them.

Another argument is whether these moves serve a public that has a limited appetite for economic updates, versus traders, who would attach a body camera and a bell to the Governor if they could. The Bank has the eight meetings a year, another half dozen or so speeches with press conferences, four parliamentary hearings, and other panel appearances. They also release quarterly business and consumer confidence surveys and a semi-annual financial system review. How much does the public really need to know?

Here I do make the distinction between a "faux transparency" of talking all the time but saying very little, and genuine engagement. We're all aware of the idea of political "talking points," and that can happen in economic policy too.

One area where I do see a problem is with private speeches given by the bank to groups of investors or private bank economists. Given the potential for profit from these meetings, I'm not sure why they happen. (Bank officials have said that the meetings are helpful for gathering information and no market-moving information is shared.) Governors, of course, have all sorts of latitude for private meetings with commercial bank CEOs, academics, and so on, so ideas can be exchanged in private and that's a good thing. But the idea of a private speech to a big group of bankers doesn't sit well, and I sense ego is being put over good practice.

CHAPTER THREE

Crisis Management 2020

It may be difficult for future generations to understand how severe a crisis the Covid-19 pandemic was when it broke open in 2020. Many lives were lost in Canada and around the world, especially vulnerable seniors in care homes, and most of the country was ordered to stay at home for weeks on end, wear masks when they went outside, and to stay at least six feet away from other people. The lost human contact was made little better by our ability to stream movies and shows in our own homes.

On the economic front, the pandemic revealed that more than eight of the thirty-five million Canadians would draw on short term "CERB" relief checks, a stark reminder that many working Canadians couldn't get by for many weeks without a paycheck. A quarter of employees shifted to working at home, opening debate about whether workers ever needed to go back to an office full-time, something that was unthinkable beforehand. Canada's government relief spending at one point was on track to hit twenty percent of

GDP, among the strongest among nations tracked by the IMF, until the U.S. Congress went even bigger.

In some ways, the government's control of the economy was the most dominant since the first and second World Wars. Canada's opposition parties in a minority Parliament also gave the Liberals scope for almost unlimited emergency spending power. Industries like airlines and hotels suffered greatly, while a handful of grocery store chains and Amazon flourished. While vaccines were developed very rapidly, in the meantime, governments struggled with a crisis that had no playbook. The Spanish flu happened a century earlier when the economy and healthcare was radically different, and the steep recessions triggered by health lockdowns were unlike those that came as part of the regular business cycle. In short, the economy was controlled for more than a year by the pandemic, over everything else.

Profiting from the lessons of 2008 and moving fast

The events over the period I'm writing about make it clear to me there are two types of policies—those set in regular times and those set in times of crisis.

Several times during 2020, I was struck by the fact that my career started with a scenario that, at the time, seemed so dire, and now seems almost cute: the Y2K crisis that was going to take out all our computers. The recent impeachment trial of Bill Clinton had raised questions about the degradation of media standards and a weakening of democracy. In 2020, we were now looking at the impeachment of Donald Trump and the degradation of media, plus a global recession.

Between these two events was the 2008 financial crisis, which was another long test of mettle covering financial markets; every day we waited to see if a domestic institution would fail or something else equally bad would happen.

Once I had 9/11 and 2008 under my belt, I had the delusion that I had covered the "Once in a Century" events that I would be using to lecture other reporters about for the rest of my career. Little did I know 2020 was still coming.

I have learned that we don't profit in our work by being on high alert all the time, and I realize that, as one person or bureau, we will miss covering a few big stories the second they happen. What we can do is know when we really have to sprint, and when to slow it down, and not become too convinced that every day will have some major bad news.

The year 2020 made newsgathering almost completely digital in a way it wasn't before, despite the hype. While some TV reporters went to socially distanced press conferences in person, the government now took half the questions over the phone. Reports that previously came only by way of an in-person lockup were now emailed on the honour system, or with a password. Luckily, I had already been working two or three days a week at home.

When I look back at 2020, I see that policy makers clearly learned the lessons from past economic crises—act early and aggressively—unlike the 1930s, and the inconsistent response to 2008-09. In a year with a risk of deflation—why wouldn't prices fall with everyone locked up for a month— they only fell for two months.

Monetary policy quickly moved to near-zero interest rates, and emergency tools like holding rates low, doing whatever it takes, and making some forms of asset purchases for the first time. Governments had no hesitation rolling out record budget deficits and targeting most of the direct cash aid to households. If we look at the other two big economic indicators—unemployment and economic growth—while joblessness peaked near a postwar record of fourteen percent, it also started falling again when things reopened, a sign that firms and consumers still had confidence in the future. GDP had a dramatic fall, but snapped back. Stimulus policies clearly helped prevent an economic collapse.

Through late January and early February, I remember thinking that the virus wasn't a big deal, and that Canada had learned so much from SARS (a 2003 pandemic that Canada largely contained) that we would do much better than everyone else. We didn't. By the end of the year, I was discouraged by so many reports about how the government perhaps had let its guard down.

It's hard to relate to people who didn't live it the toll of being isolated, by law, for at least two months of that year, and under ever-changing restrictions the rest of it, has on everyone. I worked at home, save for two or three days, for the rest of 2020. For an official Ottawa built on press conferences, briefings, lockups, and photo ops, the lockdowns and restrictions made things hard. Things have slowly shifted back to normal, but it's still awkward to be in a closed room with people, or to be in any large crowd. Most federal civil servants are also still working at home, making Ottawa different than most other Canadian cities.

After the toughest lockdown, there was a still a bit of a lag on data proving how bad the recession would be. This was the year people opened the spigots on real-time data, after many years of hyping big data as an economic miracle with few tangible results. Statistics Canada published flash estimates much faster than usual, and they were highly accurate most of the time. The Canadian Federation of Independent Business published a biweekly survey of 500 firms. Google travel data became a big deal.

One personal story of the human cost: my wife put an old bunk bed up for offer on a free website, and the person claiming it told her he needed it because three families were moving into one house to save cash after they were laid off.

I had one drink in the local bar in 2020, the day before the lockdown came, thinking of it as a joke—it was the end of that for a while. It certainly was. The next drink, after the one in February, was in July, when outdoor drinking was briefly allowed in Ottawa. It was odd that we were pushing twenty-something workers back into the workplace under such conditions, to work for tips. I also wanted more like twenty feet of space around me, and when I went out, I had plenty of space most of the time. Physical menus were gone to avoid contamination; we used bar codes on phones or just asked what was on offer.

The lockdown phase meant working at home, but the intensity of the economic disruption meant I was much busier than normal. Every day I was glued to my laptop for fear of missing major news. In one of the early months, there was more than one announcement a day on the Bank's financial markets web page, which, in another time, might have gone more than a month without a new post.

Bank of Canada Governor Stephen Poloz held several press conferences, including one with Finance Minister Bill Morneau; in normal times, this is something that only happened when a new guy was brought in. The comical thing was the dance of stressing that the Bank of Canada was still independent, because at that point, people appreciated the solidarity at a time when US President Trump was calling Jay Powell a fool, and undermining the much-needed international economic coordination.

Canada's interest rates went back to about zero, or 0.25 percent, to be precise. Funny thing was, the Bank called this the "effective lower bound" even though we all remembered a 2015 paper under Poloz where they said rates could go as low as negative 0.5 percent. He never really bridged that logic for us, other than to say that he now thought it would be a problem to take rates negative.

Less controversial than the potential bad public reaction to negative interest rates was bond purchases, known as quantitative easing. After mostly avoiding buying such assets around the 2008 financial meltdown, this time the Bank of Canada went in with at least five billion dollars per week of federal bonds. They also made a host of other asset purchases to stabilize markets: provincial paper, corporate bonds, and provincial bonds. This raised questions about political conflict and exit strategy, but again, at the time, few people cared.

The idea was that as private investors became potentially jittery about lending so much money so fast to governments and companies desperate to raise cash to tide them over, the Bank of Canada's buying up of assets was a signal all would be well.

The Bank later slowed the asset purchases to four billion dollars a week, and moved the purchases more to longer-term debt.

Breaking the glass: quantitative easing

So what is QE, or quantitative easing? Before 2008, it was seen as a nuclear option. Now it was just another part of the toolkit.

Policy makers touting QE in 2020 often left out this important detail. Many experts who witnessed its use in 2008 thought the policy had little power to turn around an economy. Central bankers who turned to QE also refused to say that cutting interest rates towards zero would also have less punch. Consumers and firms had already been borrowing on the cheap for a long time. When interest rates were six percent, if you cut them to three percent, that's a big deal. Cutting from one percent to 0.25 percent isn't as big a deal. Another sign of the weakness of rate cuts was the fact companies failed to substantially boost investment, while consumers cashed in to buy more expensive houses.

This is another example of the problem of the transmission mechanism in monetary policy, and why a crisis often demands radical action. A central bank that cuts interest rates and doesn't get more oomph into the economy is in big trouble.

So when you cut the key interest rate from one percent down to 0.25 percent, and you know the economy needs more stimulus, then what?

The historic lender of last resort idea sets up the idea of "quantitative easing." Easing: meaning getting the good stuff into the financial system. Quantitative: to mean that with interest rates stuck at zero, the only way to make it more attractive to borrow and lend is to target the quantity of cash in the system. This happens by buying up bonds in financial markets at a certain pace, meaning in effect, that banks and investors get something like cold hard cash for selling assets they may have significant doubts about anyway.

The hope is to make sure the ladder of interest rates declines further after overnight interest rates go as low as possible. Because the Bank has no direct control over interest rates on a five or ten-year bond yield, the indirect move is to buy enough of them to push down those yields. In Canada, where most of the moves in yields trade the dominant U.S debt market, this can be difficult. But not impossible.

You can ask yourself whether the Bank of Canada should have flushed something like half a trillion dollars into the financial system, just to pull down bond yields that were already at very low levels. But you can also say that if the Bank hadn't shown it was throwing the kitchen sink at this Covid-19 recession, it would have caused a deep loss of confidence. This is one big difference between regular and crisis policy. There is no room for "subtle" or "underdoing it." Still, half a trillion dollars?

Gluing it back together: Bond-buying exit plan

One thing I couldn't answer at the end of 2020 was: what is the exit plan? Other major central banks in Japan, the U.S., and Europe seemed to struggle to fully unwind their bond purchase programs. This can leave less "firepower" for the next downturn, and it leaves the bond programs as open-ended policies that some economists feel are ineffective in the first place. Besides, it raises perceptions of yet another kind of hidden bailout for big investors, backed by public resources, or subject to continued attacks as a hidden backstop for government deficits.

Would we in Canada ever get out? Soon after the Bank began raising interest rates, Governor Macklem said he would not pursue active sales of bonds on its books, but would just let the bonds on its books come to maturity. As interest rates rise quickly in 2022 (at the time of writing), it's possible that we even see another recession before we get anywhere near unwinding the bond purchases.

While there's broad agreement that "laissez-faire" free market policies made the Great Depression of the 1930s much worse, there may also need to be thinking about limits on how far a central bank should go to avoid a recession, even a very deep one, if the cost is a persistently bloated balance sheet.

Today, central banks seem unwilling to normalize monetary policy to save their power for later, sort of the opposite of past leaders, who were willing to even force a recession to break the back of inflation. Put another way, if the economy is bound for slow growth and low inflation, and the main problem is still the business cycle, why not move rates up and accept slow growth? You are using the power of monetary policy to fight a recession at every point in the economic cycle. It would be like the government saying they will run big deficits until economic growth returns to what it was in the 1960s. That being impossible, all you get is the added economic imbalance of bad fiscal policy. To say it bluntly: just as Canada learned the hard way in the 1990s that you can't run deficits forever, will we learn the hard way that you also can't keep stimulative monetary policy forever?

Politically, in 2020, even the Conservatives accepted big spending from the Liberals. Yet the Liberals, even in this atmosphere, went too far, trying to sneak through legislation giving it even more emergency spending powers beyond Parliament's oversight, in 2020 until late in 2021. Then they continued to back sending out two thousand dollar a month checks (known as CERB), under minor pressure from the NDP. The stimulus was arguably too rich, at one point leaving about one hundred billion dollars in liquid assets in Canadians' accounts. Net worth after taxes had a record increase in the middle of the pandemic.

So while policy was generous, it was not always well focused. While the Canada Emergency Response Benefit (CERB) checks went out, the first stab at a wage subsidy was well short of the seventy-five percent rate being rolled out in Europe. For anyone who wondered about the incentive to work, and keep employees over pure relief checks, this weaker wage subsidy cost jobs and confidence while boosting relief payouts that had little such long-term benefit.

Still, some form of relief was needed in the crisis. This is, in part, because governments allowed gig workers to get paid by firms who were not required to participate in the employment insurance system or other parts of our social safety net. There were more than eight million CERB applications. This tells us we are living in a society that lacks the tools to help people.

One lesson from all this is that while central banks may need extraordinary tools in a crisis, there can also be danger in being drawn into programs that may later be seen as partisan or outside their proper function. Some thought must be given to how to help, while keeping out of the fray.

Economists also point to the idea of "moral hazard" and particularly in financial markets. The idea being, once people get the idea that the government can bail them out, they may take risks or do other bad things because they will never pay the full price of their actions.

When the stimulus becomes a blur

The year 2020 was a blur well into August, in no small part because the government didn't bring in even a fiscal "snapshot" until mid-July. Then Bill Morneau was dropped from cabinet and Chrystia Freeland came in, and she pressed ahead with major fiscal stimulus.

For me, the scary moment of the year in markets was the report that even the U.S. government bond market was becoming illiquid in the spring. This was supposed to be impossible. Seemingly, people were so scared that they wanted hard cash, even over bedrock U.S. government debt. This also happened in Canada. This was another argument for quantitative easing, just to flush cash into the system. That was scary and just another moment, that in normal times, would have been a dominant story for a year; in this year, it was just one drop in the river of tears.

At first, I remember the Fed downplaying the recession, saying there could be a second half rebound. The Bank of Canada wasn't that bad, but it also seemed to give up on regular forecasts, moving to the badly-named "central planning scenario."

Governor Poloz also chided the media a few times for making false comparisons to the Great Depression. Frankly, it was hard not to compare the magnitude of the problems to those of the 1930s, even though, of course, there was no chance of bread lines in 2020.

Even with all the fiscal relief, unemployment went to a record high in modern-day records. The danger at that point was a repeat of what happened in the Great Depression, a sort of cascading series of shocks to the economy and financial system that went on for years. Early in the pandemic, the general public didn't know how fast vaccines could be developed and delivered, and later, there was growing public anger about repeated lockdowns and extended health restrictions. Business groups were reporting that smaller firms were making weekly, if not daily, decisions about shutting their doors for good. Even sound economic policy may not have been able to overcome a truly extended health crisis.

One thing that surprised me in media coverage and public attention was the intense focus on restaurants and bars. While they were certainly vulnerable, this had always been a tough business. I have seen industry figures suggesting that, even in good times, a high proportion of locations go under in their first few years of operations. Economists see the industry as pretty close to "perfect competition." That means that among other things, it's very easy to get into the business and the profit margins are never very high. I don't think it was ever possible to design a sound policy to keep them in business.

As a parent, it was also frustrating to watch a debate that, at times, pitted the need to keep businesses open against keeping schools open. And then deciding on opening the bars.

Comparing 2020 and 2008

Before continuing to talk about how policy makers responded to the pandemic, a reminder about how the Bank of Canada was born. The central bank was created in 1934, and opened its doors in 1935, as the Great Depression and other prior troubles exposed a lack of protections like deposit insurance, and the frailties of currencies issued by private banks. During colonial times, local officials even signed playing cards as a stopgap form of money to keep trade going, which shows that money can be anything people agree on to make trades efficiently.

In the Depression, stock markets crashed, banks called in some loans to try to improve their cash balances, and in the process, ruining solid businesses. Governments refused to run big deficits, as part of a wider "laissez-faire" attitude that reasoned that markets would self-correct more-quickly if left alone. Unemployment surged beyond twenty percent, creating a wider political challenge to capitalist economies around the world, and pushing some nations to extreme alternatives.

The differences in how policy makers responded to the Covid pandemic, less than a century later, are incredible. Canada ran budget deficits unseen outside of wartime, interest rates were cut to zero, and central bank officials even briefly considered whether negative interest rates could be helpful. The government announced that people could defer six months of mortgage payments, and discouraged evictions and foreclosures. In short, there was no merit seen in letting people fill up soup kitchens, standing idle while businesses failed, or trying to keep a balanced budget.

Even in 2008, when the U.S. suffered a banking and economic crisis, Canada advanced several programs to make sure our financial system kept running as smoothly as possible. This was under Conservative Finance Minister Jim Flaherty.

Early in the pandemic, Canada went further by beginning to buy up government bonds, the "quantitative easing" described earlier. At first, Bank of Canada Governor Stephen Poloz was reluctant to call it quantitative easing, but he was later more candid about it. Not so many years earlier, such a move was known as "unconventional monetary policy," and now it was taking centre stage.

Other pandemic tools included purchases of assets such as treasury bills, corporate bonds, provincial bonds, and the central bank buying up a bigger share at auctions.

At the same time, there were some ideas that Canada never took on. When push came to shove, Governors Poloz and Macklem judged that negative interest rates could backfire. While buying some corporate and provincial government debt, a potential political minefield, the programs, in the end, were fairly small and generic. The Bank of Canada also declined to use a policy known as "yield curve control." That is when a central bank decides to set a target range for bonds of a specific maturity, like debt due in five years, aiming to spur business lending at lower costs, and hopefully boosting economic growth. One lesson to draw from this is that, even in a crisis, there are some moves that are likely unworkable, unpopular, or which have a high risk of backfiring.

Extraordinary action to keep the financial system running was more palatable in 2020 because Covid was more of a "blameless crisis," compared to 2008, when people blamed reckless bankers. This time, banks were seen playing a much more positive role in keeping loans flowing to entrepreneurs who needed financing to carry them through the lockdowns. The pandemic also hit across most industries, and unlike 2008, there was no focus on industries like banks or automakers getting special bailouts. Rather, the question was quickly producing more of some goods like medical gloves, hand sanitizers and vaccines, no matter the cost.

We clearly learned many lessons from the 1930s, which were implemented in 2020, with fast and strong stimulus. One debate lingering today from the experience of 2008 is how fast to pull back the fiscal and monetary stimulus. After 2008, some governments closed the stimulus taps quite early in the recovery, and there was a feeling that that led to a decade of very weak economic growth. Through the pandemic, policy makers talked of "having people's backs" until we were well through it, and the rapid inflation of 2022 is now being blamed on fiscal and monetary policy that overdid the stimulus.

The wear and tear on the people running the economy showed itself as many top economic officials left: Bill Morneau left; as did the innovation minister, in early 2021; Governor Poloz decided to go ahead with a scheduled retirement; the head of OSFI said he would retire; the head of CMHC extended his term, but left early in 2021; and the Governor General, in early 2021, who would have to be consulted if there was a move to a snap election. Imagine a major corporation losing so much executive talent in a year.

At the same time, it was striking that all the new leaders embraced the policies of the outgoing leaders. Maybe leaders of institutions are really just like corks, bobbing on top of the waves, and most decisions really bubble up from staff and evidence; perhaps by the time the boss gets to the meeting, the options are around a narrow band of things to consider. They can tweak it and call it their own, but maybe anyone else would have done about the same. The fact that

Canada's economic recovery has carried on with so many top officials leaving suggests that there is a deep bench of talent, and this kind of development needs to continue as a best practice for managing future emergencies.

The quiet heroes of OSFI

One strength of Canada over the U.S. in both 2008 and 2020 is having a standalone and fairly stern bank regulator, OSFI.[1] OSFI works on a basis of principles rather than legalistic rules that banks could try to "lawyer" their way around. I also felt banks in Canada have a genuine fear of the regulatory hammer coming down on them if they step offside. For sound crisis management, it's worth considering how much power should be put under the roof of any one agency, and how to coordinate the work of the different agencies to keep them all effective. Some have said that Canada's relatively small number of banks, relatively sheltered from global takeovers and competition, are more able to play things safe.

A taste for deficits?

On the fiscal side, it's an open question where we stand along the spectrum between chronic deficits leading up to the fiscal nightmare of the 1990s and the discipline we showed afterwards. Before the pandemic, the public shifted to tolerate Prime Minister Trudeau's modest deficits, then his stripping away of any real fiscal targets, then the commitment to keep adding deficits as the economy got back on its feet. Will we develop a sweet tooth for deficits?

This is a good place to again remind everyone who worries about Canada's finances getting out of control, that the one real check on Canada in the bad times leading up to the 1990s was the threat from global bond investors and rating companies that Canada would be shut out of financial markets, and unable continue to raise more cash.

This time, markets are telling us just the opposite. Canada still generally has top ratings. Interest rates that investors charge the government to borrow fell to record lows, even as the deficit went to record highs. The public budget office has said that, even with our massive deficits around Covid, and stimulus

---

1   Office of the Superintendent of Financial Institutions

the IMF calls the strongest among major economies, at twenty percent of GDP, our debt servicing ratio will still fall to a record low. The government is also selling more long-term bonds to make sure we keep this advantage, even if interest rates rise in the future.

Of course, what markets give, they can take away, meaning there is a danger of assuming that low interest rates will persist for a long time and that governments shouldn't worry about deficits that much.

CHAPTER FOUR

Selected Turning Points 2000-2020

Before turning to the broader history of the Bank of Canada's actions over the period from 2000 to 2020, I'd like to quickly boil down a few of the most dramatic events, and whether the Bank did it right.

The unscheduled rate cut in 2001 after the 9/11 attacks

It seems clear they had to do it, and they had the freedom to pull some of it back later. The Bank of Canada arguably got the idea of a surprise move out of the way shortly after moving to fixed announcement dates, thereby ending what could have been months of unhelpful speculation by investors about an unscheduled move coming. The unscheduled move is also a helpful reminder to investors and the public that, while it's usual to stick to its eight scheduled meetings a year, the BOC does have the option of being more flexible when needed. The fast rate cuts were also widely credited afterwards with helping Canada avoid the worst of the U.S. downturn, and the domestic economy's resilience was also a welcome surprise after all the painful adjustments of the 1990s, as Canada slashed the federal deficit.

The unexpected rate cut in 2015 followed by another one a few months later

The Bank was right to act, but it was a pyrrhic victory, given that it lost some trust with markets for years afterwards. Governor Stephen Poloz had a strong point when he said it wasn't his job to hand-feed market analysts who are paid to come to their own conclusions. It was also true that, just by looking at the collapse of the price of oil before the rate cut, which was among Canada's biggest export products, the rate reduction should not have been a major surprise. Still, you must admit that at least a small part of the Bank's job is keeping credibility with markets. Poloz's paper about not using code words was laid out only a short while before he put it into practice, and markets were perhaps owed a little more time to adjust.

Mark Carney's rate hikes after the global financial crisis and his "conditional commitment" to hold rates

Carney arguably broke his pledge to hold rates a bit early, but he was wise to see that markets wouldn't care much, and it helped him with the task of calming hot housing markets and giving the Bank more room to cut in the next downturn. (Remember Carney worked at Goldman Sachs, so he had a good handle on market reactions.) At the same time, he left perceptions about a bias to tighten rates on Poloz's shoulders and he wasn't able to follow through given the economy's needs at the time. If Carney had stayed on, would markets have noticed? Finally, is there a benefit to sticking fully to a conditional commitment to make that kind of tool more powerful in the future?

Risking dreaded "one-sided bets" in markets

Governors did see that promising low rates for a long time, or even just holding them low without a promise, would warp financial markets and how Canadians handled their own finances. It has also encouraged aggressive trading in stock markets and other assets like housing. While warning of a risky "search for yield" by investors, it's also the rational outcome of a world where you don't make much money in safe bonds. Even our pension funds have moved from traditional strategies to make a decent return. Other investors find it less costly to borrow money to push into the stock market, and still more just don't see the bond market as an option at all. By becoming such a key guarantor of low interest rates, the Bank of Canada makes itself a bit irrelevant when warning about asset bubbles. Why listen to a Governor warning about dangerous financial markets when he is never willing to do anything about it? So perhaps conditional commitments have benefits in times of panic, but they also carry risks of a loss of credibility when they are broken. The Bank can also create problems if the commitments last too long, create complacency, or backfire by signalling too much pessimism to the public.

The car insurance head fake

Markets often cheekily go on about "policy errors": moving interest rates when you shouldn't and having to take it back. I've never met anyone in the real world who has accused the Bank of this, so maybe we in media and financial markets can retire this phrase.

However, after a nudge up in core inflation, David Dodge raised rates in March and April of 2003 to 3.25 percent, after a run up in total inflation led by energy, but also a rise in "core" inflation that, at the time, excluded eight items and a few indirect taxes. (Since then, the Bank has moved to new core inflation measures, trying to better capture the real trend of prices. This hasn't been a total success either.)

As it turns out, Dodge himself noted in a June 2003 speech that a spike in auto insurance rates had pushed up core inflation. The standard textbook of central banking advises to ignore one-off rises in inflation, but to react to broad-based persistent gains in consumer prices. The core rate was supposed to help sort out the narrow energy-driven inflation that often faded away from the persistent and more dangerous times.

In the June 2003 speech, Dodge said, "But even allowing for the extraordinarily large increases in insurance premiums, inflation was well above target," even as he noted longer-term inflation expectations remained around two percent.

To be fair, 2003 was a messy year for the economy, as Dodge pointed out, with the SARS[2] virus coming into the country, and the BSE[3] outbreak hurting beef production. There was also an Ontario electricity rebate—another one-off price swing. Canada's dollar was also coming off record lows in 2002, creating inflation through more expensive imports.

The record shows that the Bank was soon looking to cut rates way back down to two percent. This resulted in a rare case of going from rate hikes to rate cuts within a couple of meetings, outside of a recession.

At the first cut in July the announcement said, "the Bank still expects that growth in the Canadian economy will strengthen towards the end of 2003 and through 2004." In September, the statement noted core inflation had fallen faster than expected.

One thing that stands out is that insurance rates are heavily regulated and sometimes move in jolts, so they could go on the list of things to overlook when it comes to trend inflation.

---

2   SARS: severe acute respiratory syndrome (another in the family of coronaviruses)

3   BSE: bovine spongiform encephalopathy, a progressive neurological disorder in cattle

CHAPTER FIVE

The Main Trail, Part One

Having gone through the high-level issues, this chapter walks through the eight interest-rate decisions that led from high interest rates to record low rates in the span of one year, and from economic booms to busts. Looking back over this period helps us understand the details of crisis policy versus regular policy, and a shift from high to low rates.

No more surprises: A shift away from shocking the market

One major improvement to communications from the Bank came just as this era started, and when I started my career. I was there for one of the last interest-rate changes that was done under the old system, where the bank reserved the right to change the policy rate at 9 a.m. each business day without any announcement. The Bank's trading desk seemed to just go into the market and make trades to push interest rates to where they wanted them, without really telling anyone directly. The only way even Bloomberg found out was they had a couple of veteran reporters who would try to remember to check each morning, especially when a rate change was seen as coming; they would have to look at some money market screenshots and see if there was a jolt. It was usually an obvious vertical line up or down to the new level. I was never really involved in that. One day, my editor came up to me and explained that one of these moves had just happened. I then had to frantically call trading desks and they would all say what had happened. My vague memory is that the bank generally wouldn't confirm things immediately.

Try to imagine doing this with fiscal policy. The Finance Minister drops a copy of the federal budget in the lobby of parliament, without telling anyone, and walks away.

The thinking back then was that monetary policy was more effective if you didn't tell anyone what you were doing. This certainly put markets ahead of the public. But was it beneficial? I doubt it. The move, around 2000, to "fixed announcement dates" was a big deal—we hardly even think about being any other way now. Greater transparency is a top benefit. I think the bank sees that greater dialogue even helps them map out a better course.

Having fixed days also takes some pressure off the Bank of Canada to potentially respond to sudden but perhaps fleeting economic events. The bank has now built up a detailed working plan—economic research papers, staff meetings, and timing the meeting dates each year to come at times when they often have the right flow of economic data in front of them, like a recent inflation report or the latest quarterly GDP figures. This has worked so well, there have been very few times they have had to move outside regular meeting dates, and in those cases it's clearly visible why they had to move, as in the 2020 pandemic. Markets clearly like the ability to prepare as well. There is much more market commentary and views given in the run-up to decision dates than there ever could be under a surprise scenario. And you remove the cottage industry of trying to guess when a surprise change was coming.

Rate hikes towards six percent, never to be seen again

The first press release about an interest-rate decision in 2000 was a move on Feb. 3, an increase to 5.25 percent. And the decision said—out loud—that the move came a day after the Fed also made a quarter point increase, the kind of comparison the Bank would later often seek to avoid as it asserted its independence. The statement did also say the decision was made based on what was best for the domestic economy.

In May, the key rate was raised by half a point to 5.75 percent, warning of inflation pressures spilling over from the U.S. Those were different times.

In September 2000, the Bank made the switch from the practice of potentially moving rates on any day as a matter of policy to a system where they would make announcements on eight fixed dates each year. They noted that many other major central banks had already been working under this more regular system.

In December 2000, the Bank rate was raised to six percent, with inflation near the top of its one-to-three percent target band.

Little did I know that I would never again see these dizzying heights over the next twenty years—and counting. And it seemed even more impossible that within a decade we would accept a near zero rate, and in 2020 we would be speculating about whether Tiff Macklem would take us to a negative interest rate in the second or third wave of a pandemic.

The year closed with the Dec. 20 announcement that David Dodge would be Governor as of Feb. 1, 2001, following Gordon Thiessen. In another sign of the times, the press release noted that Dodge had previously worked on the Anti-Inflation Board. Trying to start that kind of a board today seems almost impossible given how heavy-handed it would look.

2001: Thiessen walks away, Dodge inherits bad times

In January 2001, I covered Gordon Thiessen's last speech at the Royal York hotel in Toronto. My strongest memory is watching him walk into the sunset, so to speak. After his speech to a big crowd, I saw him walking in the underground tunnel heading north, with no aides around him, alone. To me, it was a nice antidote to today's celebrity culture.

Dodge gave his first speech in February of 2001 in Toronto. At the time, Dodge clearly had his eye on the damaging inflation of the 1970s and 1980s. Specifically, "the ups and downs in output and employment, and the waste of valuable economic resources as they are diverted from productive investments to speculative activities. All of this should be enough to strengthen our collective resolve not to let inflation break out again."

In March, Dodge cut the key rate half a point to 5.25 percent. In hindsight, the striking thing is that even in the new era of transparency, the commentary was three paragraphs long, 266 words. The January 2021 commentary was six paragraphs long, 612 words.

In April, Dodge lowered the key rate (back then known as the "Bank rate," and now the "target rate on overnight loans between commercial banks") by a quarter point to five percent. He cut the rate, even with inflation around three percent, because it was projected to fade to two percent by the end of the year. This was the era of the dot com bubble and a slowdown in both the Canadian and U.S. economies.

Again, it's important to remember that when the Bank changes interest rates today, the bulk of the effect comes about a year after the fact, so to be perfectly right, they have to have a very good sense about where inflation is headed.

Even with the fixed schedule of dates to announce policy, sometimes it leaves policy makers to make big decisions just days before or after the government presents a budget, Canada reports the latest inflation figures, the U.S. economy changes course, or financial markets spasm. And of course, a year from now, no one will remember that the difficult judgment made under partial information, they will only remember that inflation is now off target.

During this time, the bank's major economic forecast, published in the Monetary Policy Report (MPR), did not come out on the same day as the rate decision. Investors often reacted to the rate announcement in one way, then when the MPR came out, place a very different bet. This was not a healthy thing. Eventually the production time, including translation, was smoothed out; the Monetary Policy Report now appears at the same time as the rate decision.

With signs that Canada's economy was already slowing a bit, the Bank cut the policy rate a quarter point to four percent on Aug. 28th. Of course, 2001 is remembered for little else beyond the Sept. 11 terrorist attacks in the U.S. But the relatively quick recovery of Canada's economy to that shock is even more remarkable given it wasn't in top form before these attacks.

The 9/11 attacks brought the "lender of last resort" function of the Bank to the fore. The job of a central bank is to backstop commercial lending channels in a panic. The Bank stated that day: "In light of the tragic events in the United States, the Bank of Canada would like to assure the public that it will provide the liquidity necessary to support the stability of the Canadian financial system and the continued functioning of financial markets."

I remember, for days, talking to traders about the uncertainty about key market infrastructure working, key staff having disappeared, and whether trades across time zones would keep moving at all.

As someone who officially ranks myself as a coward—I never wanted to cover violence, and therefore, I thought business reporting would do nicely—I was not prepared to make the calls I had to make in the days after 9/11. Currency and bond trading was still going on for urgent orders, so I had to make the calls. Every conversation began with an apology, asking how you were doing, maybe listening in case they wanted to talk about someone they knew who was killed. Thanking them for talking, saying it's a difficult time, hanging up. Everyone was gracious and professional. I had gone to school at Columbia University in New York a few years earlier, so it felt more personal. In the pandemic of 2020, there is a similar etiquette of asking everyone you talk to about how they are coping, if they've been vaccinated, if they've been out of the house lately.

While, in 2020, there was angst about whether the dash to cash would harm even the U.S. Treasury market, it just wasn't the same grief and absence of order we saw in 2001.

On Sept. 14, the Bank reported, "Canada's payments, clearing, and settlement systems have functioned well this week."

Then, on Sept. 17, the real slide began. The bank cut rates half a point to 3.5 percent, moving outside its only recently-adopted fixed schedule for announcements.

About a month later, the big one: a three-quarter point cut in the key rate, to 2.75 percent.

The bank noted that there was already economic weakness even before the terrorist attacks, and the attack made this trend much worse.

There was another half point cut on Nov. 27, then another quarter point on Jan. 15, 2002, to two percent. This meant that in "real" terms; that is, after accounting for inflation, the interest rate was effectively zero if inflation was at target. Of course, the bank said that day that inflation was at 0.7 percent, so in fact, even that low interest rate was still arguably restrictive.

In March, the downward slide slowed. The bank held its key rate at two percent. "While uncertainties remain, the Bank expects the economy to gather strength as the year progresses."

In April, it raised the rate a quarter point, saying "A robust recovery appears to be underway in Canada," and making a similar move in June, and again in July.

Canada was avoiding a recession that was seen hitting the U.S., something almost unheard of, after generations of Canada following or lagging the world's largest economy. Given the tough times of the 1990s, this was clear evidence that Canada's economy had undergone a durable transformation. Otherwise, there was no question that the economic weakness following the 9/11 attacks would have hurt us very badly.

Flirting with U.S. dollarization

With the economy back on a surer path, Dodge had the task in October of speaking in Sherbrooke, Quebec, about "Dollarization and North American Integration." It's hard to remember today, but around this era there were some high-profile questions about the Canadian dollar's usefulness. Some people even thought adopting the U.S. dollar might be better for our trade-dependent economy, and perhaps really an effort to be inside "Fortress America."

Today, the Bank is so confident about the Canadian dollar's role as an economic shock absorber, it pre-announced that the floating currency would stay in its next five-year policy decision.

Even at the time, it was a bit strange to think about giving up the Canadian dollar when we just had real evidence that independent monetary policy could keep us out of a U.S. recession. Dodge did the standard job of showing why we need a floating currency for independent monetary policy to work, and how it's a useful release valve for the differences in the Canadian and U.S. economic cycles.

There was another lesson around this time in the Eurozone crisis with Greece. Experts felt the Eurozone was a case where having very different economies and fiscal policies within one currency zone was causing serious problems in countries like Greece. Canada, by taking on the U.S. dollar, would face this, not just on the level of being out of synch with the U.S. economy, but also perhaps losing some of the flexibility policy makers have to address disparities in the performance of provincial economies. And unlike in Europe, where small economies still have some representation at the central bank, Canada would likely have no say in U.S. monetary policy.

Halfway back in 2003

Around mid-2003, the Bank had raised its key rate back up to three percent, but there would soon be another mix of bad surprises. In September, the bank lowered the rate to 2.75 percent and said, "This recent weakness reflects the impact of a number of near-term factors such as severe acute respiratory syndrome (SARS), the effect of an isolated case of bovine spongiform encephalopathy (BSE) on exports of Canadian beef and cattle, the power blackout in Ontario, and the forest fires in Western Canada."

After all that turmoil, in 2006, the government and bank agreed to renew the two percent inflation target for another five years. And why not, given how well monetary policy had been carrying the economy through some bad times. Even with the overall success, these five-year agreements between the Bank and the Finance Minister keep monetary policy independent in day-to-day operations, but ensures that a democratic government stays in ultimate control. The review is one way of ensuring that neither side falls asleep at the wheel. Put another way, these agreements can also be a window for a government to tweak monetary policy without seeking to remove a Governor.

Relative tranquility in 2005

In September 2005, the bank raised rates a quarter point to 2.75 percent, another quarter point in October, and another in December. Inflation at the time was 2.6 percent. They kept going, moving another quarter point to 3.5 percent in January 2006, another move each in March, April, and May. Now we were at a recent high-water mark of 4.25 percent.

The rate hikes didn't get back to six percent, but heck, we were coming out of all those shocks of the early 2000s. At the time, if anyone was thinking about it, it could have been reasonable to think that six percent wasn't impossible if the economy kept chugging along.

The Bank's explanation at the time wasn't to call this a high-water mark for the economy, or to say this was an extremely tight rate; today, even with rapid inflation, some people argue a rate of more than four percent could cause a recession! The Bank said at the time:

> The strong momentum in the global and Canadian econo-mies has continued, although there has recently been an increased degree of volatility in commodity markets, foreign exchange markets, and financial markets more generally. Recent Canadian data confirm that domestic demand remains solid, and that both CPI and core inflation are evolving largely in line with the Bank's expectations. With today's increase, the target for the overnight rate is now at a level that is expected to keep the Canadian economy on the base-case path projected in the April Monetary Policy Report (MPR) and to return inflation to the 2 percent target.

Danger Lurked Beneath the Great Moderation

Following the American banking and housing crash around 2008 and 2009, there were questions about whether anyone had warned about such dangers or could see anything bad coming. In New York, in March 2006, Dodge gave a speech, "Global Imbalances: Why Worry? What to Do?" At the time, the focus was on current account imbalances, in essence, the U.S. running a big deficit on payments with the rest of the world, and other nations, especially in Asia, running big surpluses.

"There is every reason to believe that a market adjustment to these imbal-ances will take place," Dodge said. "If this adjustment is disorderly, it would affect the economy through a sudden drop in demand and prices and a resulting decline in economic output. It could also cause a painful correc-tion in capital markets and exchange rates. In a worst-case scenario, it could do both."

In November 2006, Dodge also spoke to a "World Hedge Funds Summit" in Vaughn, Ontario. Sign of the times!

The 2000s continued the "Great Moderation" that began in the mid-1980s because of fairly good growth and steady inflation. Rates moved around a lot. We were warned about financial imbalances, but in hindsight, it seems clear we didn't understand them and didn't stop them.

Over this era, Dodge did give several impressive speeches calling attention to the decline of stable private pension plans. I can only say, go back and read them. When we look at 2020, the instability around the social safety net, what we know about our aging population, and the generational angst between well-off boomers and struggling millennials, pensions are a big deal.

Dodge looked at how corporations, and the governments who regulate them, were pulling out of many defined benefit pensions. Recently, the government has sought to repair this by expanding the Canada Pension Plan. There are trade-offs to this, because it takes away the financial choices of people who don't need or want the standard CPP framework. In another way, it does reshape society from one of personal responsibility for retirement savings to a passive plan led by government policy. If you believe that economies should empower people to make autonomous decisions, just as democracy should empower autonomous voters, we are creating a world where the well-being of seniors is standardized. This, over time, may also create a stagnant industry when it comes to providing homecare and other seniors' services because most Canadians will have about the same spending power.

Here's a pension speech by Dodge: https://www.bankofcanada.ca/2007/05/sound-pension-system-handling-risk-appropriately/

CHAPTER SIX

The Main Trail, Part Two.

Carney as Rock Star through the U.S. housing crash

2007: No one knew this was the last year of the good times.

Around this time, Dodge said he wouldn't seek a second term. Financial reporters spent months chasing people who wouldn't talk about the selection process or potential shortlist candidates. Reporters wrote stories about the likely Governors-in-waiting, and we were all so wrong.

Mark Carney was announced as the new Governor in October 2007, effective Feb. 1, 2008. As an alum of Goldman Sachs, he would become the Man of the Hour in the public sector.

A week later, Tiff Macklem, then a Deputy Governor, moved to do a stint at the finance department. Carney had also been a Deputy Governor in 2003 for a short time before moving to the finance department in 2004. These things would only feed media and market speculation that "outside experience" was trumping the traditional climb up the internal ladder in the Bank of Canada that had been in place before Dodge. That is, every Governor before Dodge has been promoted from within. It also raised a logical question about central bank independence from the finance department, but it's never been at all clear this was an issue. However, perceptions matter, and you can ask yourself today about such direct ties between the finance department and a central bank that is buying billions of dollars a week in federal government bonds.

Still, in the major crisis created by the pandemic, questions about the potential political dangers of cooperation between the government and the central bank were far less important than taking the actions needed to save the economy from a free-fall.

At the same time, central bank independence is a hard-won concept that needs to outlast any activist government. While there is an exit plan, today we remain far from the end of the Bank's bond purchase program.

Flattering ties, annoying questions

Let me give you the real dish on Carney: he liked a nice tie. More importantly, Carney's mind was fast enough to remark on those things while you were sitting down, and by the time that was done, he had figured out the entire room. Sometimes you could see his face shift before someone had finished delivering a question or argument, and you hoped he was going to agree with it rather than shred it.

Of course, all Governors were smart, and even without that, I have learned one of the worst things you could hear at a press conference is, "That's a great question," because that was often code for, "Give me five seconds to dig up something that saves us all from further foolishness."

Or, as Stephen Poloz once growled at me, just after telling my summer student why it was important to ask good, tight, questions: "Is that your question?" Or a colleague who heard, "Have you seen Chart Six?" in other words, did you read anything we just published?

Over time, reporters are annoying, so getting some pushback is part of the game. I am more impressed by the dozens of very odd questions that Governors scoop up and run with.

Smoke from next door

At the end of 2007, the key interest rate was lowered a quarter point to a still healthy 4.25 percent. We could now see the smoke coming from the house next door: The statement from that decision said: "Downside risks to the Bank's inflation projection have increased. Global financial market difficulties related to the valuation of structured products and anticipated losses on U.S. sub-prime mortgages have worsened since mid-October, and are expected to persist for a longer period of time. In these circumstances, bank funding costs have increased globally and in Canada, and credit conditions have tightened further. There is an increased risk to the prospects for demand for Canadian exports as the outlook for the U.S. economy, and in particular the U.S. housing sector, has weakened."

Dodge's last speech as Governor, in December 2007, was about what would scar the world for a decade, the financial crisis. A good chunk of the speech was about the trouble the Bank of Canada had seen several years earlier, and noting that we were now seeing a bigger problem. He observed:

"The increased use of leveraged structured products was pioneered in major financial centres such as New York and London, although eventually, non-bank institutions began to market these products elsewhere, including here in Canada. The ease with which these highly structured products were sold fuelled the demand for the creation of higher-risk assets, including U.S. subprime-mortgage loans. This, in turn, contributed to the global decline in lending standards."

It would be fair to ask now whether global regulators saw these toxic securities surging in the marketplace, and, if they did, why they didn't regulate to make them safe. Or why we didn't ask the age-old question of how you can suddenly make millions and billions by just repackaging existing loans? And where were the rating firms, paid to protect us from ourselves?

Dodge said, "One thing that is clear is that, in the future, credit-rating agencies will find it to their advantage to explain more clearly the rationale for, and limitations of, their ratings for highly structured products. There are some natural, self-correcting market forces at work that should lead the rating agencies to improve their processes."

The speech also didn't really sound an alarm bell about what was coming. "While there remain upside risks to inflation in Canada, all factors considered, the Bank judges that there has been a shift to the downside in the balance of risks around our October projection for inflation. In light of this shift, we lowered the target for the overnight rate last week. Before our next interest rate decision in January, we will assess all economic and financial developments and the balance of risks, and do a full projection for the economy and inflation."

Dodge did offer some parting wisdom that remains important, given questions about crisis management in 2008 and 2020.

"The first lesson is that both individuals and firms must always be prepared to adjust quickly to changing global economic circumstances. The world will evolve in ways that we cannot predict, so we must be prepared to deal with change and seize new opportunities as they arise. Perhaps even more importantly, we should not cling to activities that are no longer economically justified," he said.

Dodge did say we must also never forget to keep public finances in check. "We have all learned the importance of achieving and maintaining sustainable levels of public debt. Canadians paid a very real price in the 1990s to control the growth of public debt, and have wisely used the favourable conditions of the past decade to bring down the ratio of public debt to GDP."

Canada didn't escape entirely unscathed from the issues around troubling debt securities. In 2007, Canada's safe bond market was roiled by asset-backed commercial paper, leading to a negotiated settlement.

"The commitment by Canada's major bank CEOs to work together to support the performance and liquidity of the market for bank-sponsored asset-backed commercial paper (ABCP) is a further positive step to help re-establish well-functioning money markets in Canada. This commitment is underpinned by the strength of their financial positions, their confidence in the underlying assets, and their ongoing commitment to provide liquidity for bank-sponsored ABCP on maturity." (See: https://www.bankofcanada.ca/2007/08/bank-canada-joint-commitment/)

While Canada didn't need to use full-blown quantitative easing in 2008 as global financial markets tanked, the strains on markets like ABCP, in particular, needed special attention. This led Governor David Dodge to push for the Bank of Canada Act to be amended to greatly expand a Governor's powers to buy or sell a wide range of securities to calm markets. The Bank, under Dodge, had already pushed the envelope somewhat with some actions to keep markets functioning and the amendments formalized those actions. This legal change made the response to the market disruptions from Covid easier to implement, and they went ahead with little attention, even for higher risk securities like corporate bonds. This was different than a past approach, when most interventions were aimed at financing for very short periods and for a more conservative list of securities, such as government bills and bonds; Parliament's granting of more discretion to the Governor was a sign of more trust in the Bank and the recognition of how dangerous the 2008 crisis was. As the Bank stressed in its 2007 annual report, this assessment drew heavily on the experience of other central banks going through the crisis.

During this time, Conservative Finance Minister Jim Flaherty and Prime Minister Stephen Harper were also confronted with a very dire economy, a Bank of Canada pushing the envelope of actions it could use to could intervene in financial markets, and its ambitions for balanced budgets. They made the important decision to allow what was then a record budget deficit to support the economy, allowing fiscal and monetary policy to work together. Politicians were taking strong actions that ran counter to their regular beliefs, likely giving the looser fiscal policy extra credibility in a difficult time. Today you can walk past the Department of Finance's headquarters on Elgin Street, and see that is dedicated in Flaherty's name.

The fire next door

When this "fire" broke out in 2008, the Bank of Canada's first move was a quarter-point rate cut to four percent. Again, the starting rate was more than twice as high as it was at the beginning of the Covid pandemic, when the Bank started cutting rates from 1.75 percent.

The Bank's words at the time show how unclear the situation was, offering a mix of strength and weakness: "Financial market conditions have deteriorated since October, leading to a tightening of credit conditions in industrial countries. Given this, and a deeper, more prolonged decline in the U.S. residential housing sector, the 2008 outlook for the U.S. economy is now significantly weaker than at the time of the October MPR."

The statement also said: "Domestic demand in Canada is projected to remain strong."

Some dark clouds followed, but no indication of a major slump: "Overall, the Bank now projects weaker growth in 2008 than was expected in October, with the economy moving into modest excess supply in the second quarter of this year. Somewhat stronger growth in 2009 brings the Canadian economy back into balance in early 2010."

There was also some explicit "forward guidance" about interest rates, rare at the time. Investors who are paid a lot of money to figure out the Bank in all situations do seem to prefer a guaranteed bet on what's happening. The problem can be that markets continue to ask for more guidance, anyway. Worse yet, they cast doubt on whether the promise should have been made, whether the Governor will be able to follow through, or they argue that it was done to paper-over the fact that monetary policy is running out of regular firepower.

If a Governor thinks it's a good idea to give guidance for extra clarity, fine. But chasing market expectations is usually a bad quick fix. Going in and out of forward guidance itself can become a damaging market signal when markets and the central bank aren't of the same view.

Carney grabs the megaphone with a half-point rate cut

While Dodge cut rates in January and signaled more was to come, Carney almost immediately made an even bigger splash. The new Governor Carney cut interest rates by half a point on March 4. Most rate cuts are quarter points, and the fact that a new Governor went further in his first decision shows that he was grabbing the megaphone—making a statement about the state of the economy. More on that in a bit.

What's striking in this first speech was his casually dropping in a reference to, "the repeal of the Corn Laws in England," and somehow none of his speechwriters could tell him needed a bit more context. Maybe the reference to English Corn Laws was just foreshadowing, given Carney would later take over the Bank of England. The passages about globalization remain worth reading today, given the wave of political populism around trade.

"While it is true that this adjustment process can be, and has been, difficult for certain individuals and firms, the overall picture is quite positive," Carney said. "In countries where labour markets are flexible, displaced workers have been more able to re-skill or retrain and, on balance, find more productive employment. Since December 2002, employment in Canada's manufacturing sector has fallen by roughly 14 percent, or 320,000 jobs, while employment in other goods-producing sectors has risen by roughly 23 percent, or 382,000 jobs. Further, over the same period, employment in the services sector has risen by more than 1.4 million jobs. Average hourly earnings have increased over this period at an average annual pace of 3.3 percent. Moreover, everyone in our economy benefits from the lower cost of imports."

Economists and central bankers, and every Governor I have covered, I think, has made this argument: that free trade, on balance, creates big wins for a country, and that workers who get hurt can be made whole by governments at some point. That may be true, but today's populist anger speaks to the idea that those who face the downsides were not made whole again.

Even many experts tout lifelong learning. But I have yet to see how the symbolic fifty-year-old factory worker who loses his job is given three years of free job training, income support, and daycare to become a computer coder. It's easy for people with masters degrees and PhDs in economics to spout off about how easy it is. This is not to say that economists don't care about the "structurally unemployed." When you are looking across a whole economy, you have to focus on the whole picture, and protecting workers too much risks creating an uncompetitive and inflexible workforce, which in the long run is much more dangerous to everyone's job security. Still, there is more work to do to make sure everyone can benefit from global competition.

Stark words about the downturn

So, back to that half-point interest-rate cut. This decision contained much more forceful language about what was going on in the U.S., while noting that our economy was still working at a high rate.

"There are clear signs that the U.S. economy is likely to experience a deeper and more prolonged slowdown than had been projected in January. This stems from further weakening in the residential housing market, which is adversely affecting other sectors of the U.S. economy and contributing to further tightening in credit conditions. The deterioration in economic and financial conditions in the United States can be expected to have significant spillover effects on the global economy."

"The Bank now judges that the balance of risks around its January projection for inflation has clearly shifted to the downside, and, as a result, the Bank is lowering the target for the overnight rate. Further monetary stimulus is likely to be required in the near term to keep aggregate supply and demand in balance and to achieve the 2 percent inflation target over the medium term."

For close readers of Bank of Canada statements, this is very stark. Weakness in the U.S. spills over into the world economy. And not only did the Bank cut half a point, there was still another piece of forward guidance saying that more is likely coming in the line about further stimulus likely being required. What's more, since the Bank targets inflation, language about risks around price increases are important. Here again, they say those risks have clearly emerged. This is a cannon shot of a statement. While even at this point, few really saw the Bank cutting rates towards zero, this statement made clear that half-point moves were a likely course of action from here.

Carney's next speech, on March 13, was more on point, "Addressing Financial Market Turbulence."

On all the ways Wall Street churned out spoiled ground beef with new types of debt securities: "the borrower often became separated from the end investor by several transactions, as credit risk was repackaged, tiered, securitized, and distributed." Noting that the downfall was now something like seven months along, Carney noted, "Even months later, the opacity of these structured products has made them harder to value." Finally, those bond rating agencies that we still turn to today as a headline-grabbing guide, such as when one agency removed Canada's top rating? "The fall from grace of the rating agencies has had a significant impact because rating agencies had grown more powerful than anyone intended. Indeed, many investors seem to have performed little or no in-house credit analysis of their investments; in other words, they substituted a subscription to a ratings publication for analysis and due diligence."

Carney gave us all a little reason to hope with the last line of his speech, noting that markets would be made to reform through regulation and market discipline: "I feel very positive about Canada's medium-term prospects in such a world."

In April, Carney cut the key rate by another half percentage point, to three percent. Still holding on to optimism about our strong economy, the policy makers boldly predicted, "The Bank projects that the Canadian economy will grow by 1.4 percent this year, 2.4 percent in 2009, and 3.3 percent in 2010."

They could have put a minus sign on the first two numbers and arguably would have been closer to the truth.

Taking a breather

Now Carney was taking a bit of a breather after the rate cuts since December, which were worth 1.5 percentage points. "Some further monetary stimulus will likely be required to achieve the inflation target over the medium term. Given the cumulative reduction in the target for the overnight rate of 150 basis points since December, the timing of any further monetary stimulus will depend on the evolution of the global economy and domestic demand, and their impact on inflation in Canada."

Let's decode this one. Now the Bank signals a rate cut, but over the medium term, which clearly means not in the next four months or so, maybe even six months. The range of things that influence their decision is long, signaling they don't see any dominant trend that guarantees more action.

The Bank held the key interest rate at three percent at the meetings in June, July, and September. The bank's Monetary Policy Report for July noted that inflation would peak temporarily above four percent in the first quarter of 2009. Hard to cut rates into that outlook, given the bank's mandate.

The forecast from July also said there were big positive and negative risks for the economy. The list of financial market strains culminated with the "Lehman moment"—the failure of the Lehman Brothers investment bank on Sept. 15—that forced world leaders to essentially put an end to bank failures. In other words, they again affirmed to markets that there could be banks that were too-big-to-fail.

Before this actually happened in financial markets, the Bank's risk list was rather different, and appeared in this order: strong domestic demand, global inflationary pressure, followed by a chance of weak commodity prices, and strains in financial markets.

One thing we learned from 2008, and the Bank has said much the same, is that traditional ways of measuring the economy aren't well equipped to tackle damaged financial markets. Models of the economy typically track things like employment, output, and prices. In a sense, these models just assume financial markets work in the background. Since then, a lot of work has been done to build models that capture some of the forces we saw when a damaged lending market tanks stocks and commodity prices, and reaches deep into the economy. We learned that, like the Titanic, if you break enough watertight holds, even the strongest ship can go down. Even today, it's fair to say that economists don't understand what might happen if a small but important financial market breaks, and how far it would spread the damage.

Similarly, the challenge of setting policy for the surge of inflation after the Covid lockdowns is partly because it's difficult to model an economy that goes through such a substantial change, not only in how companies produce but how consumers behave.

Looking back at the Bank's pause over three meetings in mid-2008, you can ask yourself if, in hindsight, policy makers really had seen the balance of risks properly at the time, and understood that this wasn't the time for gradualism. What if they had kept cutting without pause? If that turned out to be wrong and, they cut with inflation so rapid already, it would look pretty bad. Cutting sooner and without pause; how much difference would that have made? Also, if they had kept cutting, would this have hurt everyone's confidence, which is just about as important as anything else in a crisis?

One big sign of trouble was a statement on Sept. 15, as the "Lehman moment" broke open—a statement that was short enough to show the danger: "The Bank of Canada is closely monitoring global market developments. The Bank welcomes the initiatives of the Federal Reserve System to provide support to U.S. financial markets. The Bank will provide liquidity as required to support the stability of the Canadian financial system and the functioning of financial markets."

Again, when the Bank has to affirm something is creditworthy, that's a sign that that standard has already been lost. As is sometimes said about politics, don't believe something until it's been officially denied.

This overshadowed the bank's other news release headline that day, "Counterfeit $100 bills circulating in the Greater Montréal Area."

Everybody cuts at once

On October 8, some major history: a globally-coordinated interest rate cut including the Bank of Canada, the Bank of England, the European Central Bank, the Federal Reserve, Sveriges Riksbank, and the Swiss National Bank.

This was shocking news, even within this crisis. The Bank of Canada's interest-rate cut was half a percentage point, coming just three months after it had laid out how balanced the risks were and said that the economy could still grow solidly this year and next. The world had changed materially since then.

The joint statement couldn't have been blunter, after an era during which most central bankers often said that the best policy for each nation would be better than trying to coordinate the global economy. "The intensification of the global financial crisis is having a marked impact on all countries."

This was amplified at a political level when the G7 Finance Ministers and central bankers put out a statement during the annual International Monetary Fund (IMF) meetings, with this notable phrase after the Lehman collapse: They pledged to "take decisive action and use all available tools to support systemically important financial institutions and prevent their failure," and "take all necessary steps to unfreeze credit and money markets and ensure that banks and other financial institutions have broad access to liquidity and funding."

Carney moved the rate again a few weeks later, with another half point cut on Oct. 21, to 2.25 percent. Again, I'll point out that this move still left the policy rate half a point above where we started in 2020 when the pandemic hit.

The circumstances Carney described were now suitably dire in the latest rate decision, though still laced with somewhat unwarranted optimism. "The associated need for the global banking sector to continue to reduce leverage will restrain growth for some time. Second, the global economy appears to be heading into a mild recession, led by a U.S. economy already in recession. Third, there have been sharp declines in many commodity prices. The outlook for growth and inflation in Canada is now more uncertain than usual."

The outlook for growth? The bank did offer another signal of more to come, though again with some resistance to the idea: "some further monetary stimulus will likely be required to achieve the 2 percent inflation target over the medium term."

One lesson from this crisis was that at rare points, the Bank of Canada may be pulled into some coordinated decision making, with either officials at home or abroad. This would happen again during the Covid pandemic.

CHAPTER SEVEN

2009, The lowest point (so far)

Giving up on a rebound

After these half-point cuts, preparing for the next scheduled decision, it seemed reasonable to think that there would be a cut of a quarter or probably half a percentage point.

The Bank went further in December, with a three-quarter point reduction, to 1.5 percent.

My practice as a reporter was to prepare for each "lockup" for a rate decision at the Bank of Canada knowing I couldn't access the web or any of my files, or contact anyone outside the room. That meant creating a file of background facts with all plausible scenarios. Even with a lot of time to review the decision in the lockup, it's always nerve-wracking to push the send button on these stories.

At this point, it was hard to stay ahead of how fast things were moving. Bosses started asking reporters to come in very early in case there was another coordinated rate cut timed to catch European and Asian markets.

Working through these early mornings through winter in Ottawa often meant literally working from dawn until dusk. This could make things difficult when an eager editor from another office asked about writing follow-up stories.

The December 2008 decision threw in the towel on economic growth. "The outlook for the world economy has deteriorated significantly and the global recession will be broader and deeper than previously anticipated. Global financial markets remain severely strained," the statement said. "While Canada's economy evolved largely as expected during the summer and early autumn, it is now entering a recession as a result of the weakness in global economic activity. The recent declines in terms of trade, real income growth, and confidence are prompting more cautious behaviour by households and businesses."

Let's note here that central banks as stewards of public trust almost never use the word recession in print, so this is an "all systems fail" message. In other cases, you might try saying the recession will be short or limited to a slump in Alberta's oil industry, for example, or Ontario automaking.

The year 2009 began with another half point cut, to the significant level of one percent. Certainly, this was the lowest in the modern era of Bank rates. The policy interest rate was now at the bottom of the Bank's target band for inflation, which is from one percent to three percent. In other words, monetary policy was now going very far to stimulate the economy. In normal times, you might consider an even-handed policy to have interest rates at two percent or a bit higher.

Now for the first time, I was asking about running out of room to cut interest rates. At the time, there hadn't been much mainstream discussion of what would happen if you went all the way to zero in Canada.

Again, the language was stark. "Heightened uncertainty is undermining business and household confidence worldwide and further eroding domestic demand. Major advanced economies, including Canada's, are now in recession."

The explicit use of the word recession and the sweeping language about the breadth of the weakness was telling. The Bank said the economy would contract 1.2 percent in 2009, with a fairly optimistic 3.8 percent gain seen for 2010.

Here's another word that central bankers hate using: deflation. That's when consumer prices broadly fall over a sustained period, at least several months. The Bank doesn't say it here, but when your inflation target is two percent and prices fall, in a policy sense, it's less about whether you call it deflation than the dangers inherent in that kind of outcome. When consumers and firms are used to prices going up two percent, any bout of falling prices could trigger a dreaded downward spiral. Just as in good times, we all line up for a nice raise every year, if prices suddenly fall, people may see wages fall and get scared, triggering round after round of price and wage reductions. Monetary policy has almost no way out of this, and this was a key force behind the very damaging economics of the 1930s.

This line from the Bank's decision is instructive in both raising the deflation spectre, while at the same time, seeking some calm. "Total CPI inflation is expected to dip below zero for two quarters in 2009, reflecting year-on-year drops in energy prices. With inflation expectations well-anchored, total and core inflation should return to the 2 percent target in the first half of 2011 as the economy returns to potential."

In this reasoning, it's almost textbook deflation. But they won't say it, and they mainly lay out this case to quickly tell us it's going away. At this point, who could know it really would go away?

Again, if you read the first line I showed about the broad recession, everything else follows from that. But markets eat up these details. The bottom line for interest-rate hounds was obviously the signal of more rate cuts to come. "The Bank will continue to monitor carefully economic and financial developments in judging to what extent further monetary stimulus will be required to achieve the 2 percent target over the medium term."

While they introduced some flexibility with the standard line about studying the economy, the message was that only a heroic turnaround would prevent more stimulus.

Downplaying deflation risk

At this point, Carney had been on the job for about a year, and he gave a speech in Halifax. Carney said that deflation, in fact, was when prices fell "year after year," as opposed to the more innocent "disinflation," a brief fling with that phenomenon. He brought home the message that inflation would turn up again soon.

Later he said that Japan's deflation had triggered a lost decade, and worries about deflation were rising in the U.S. Deflation in Canada was a "remote" possibility.

The record showed that inflation turned negative in Canada for just a month and returned to two percent at the end of 2009.

Carney correctly pointed out that Canada's banking system was sound, and still pumping out consumer and business loans. So the rate cuts he made worked somewhat normally, an advantage that other nations lacked. He also noted that the lower dollar aided exports and eased the blow from lower commodity prices. Above all, people never really expected deflation to set in, so there was little chance for a downward spiral.

Come March, Carney went as far as any Governor had done in the modern era, cutting another half point, to 0.5 percent. Again, the half point move underscored the seriousness of the situation.

Making these kinds of assessments about reaching historic lows for the key interest rate is tricky because the way policy has been made shifts over time. (See: https://www.bankofcanada.ca/core-functions/monetary-policy/key-interest-rate/)

From 1935 to 1956, the Bank Rate was set by policy makers directly, and did not change very often. From there until 1962, it was set based on treasury bill auction results, not by any active decision. Back to a fixed rate until 1980, then based on bill auction results again until 1996. Then they went back to fixing a policy rate. Clear enough? And through the 1990s, the bank also shifted from a "Bank Rate" as its policy focus, to "the target for the overnight rate."

Either way, the move to 0.5 percent was a low in the modern era.

The Bank's statement reminded us that the core of the U.S. recession in housing and consumer spending hurt our exports of autos and building materials. And we were now calling some financial securities "toxic assets." Remember when the Bank predicted a 3.8 percent rebound in economic growth in 2010? Now the Bank was saying that the gross domestic product might not even begin to move back up to its potential until early 2010. This is what's known as the "output gap," the difference between an economy at peak performance and whether it's moving too slowly and creating weak inflation pressure. In good times, you can also have an economy working so hard that inflation keeps pushing up.

And some more "forward guidance" on interest rates. When you are this close to zero, your only move is to pledge to hold them at rock bottom levels for a while. The Bank said, "the target for the overnight rate can be expected to remain at this level or lower at least until there are clear signs that excess supply in the economy is being taken up."

This, along with the near-zero rate, took monetary policy to the precipice of full-on emergency measures. "Given the low level of the target for the overnight rate, the Bank is refining the approach it would take to provide additional monetary stimulus, if required, through credit and quantitative easing."

The Bank was also playing up the totality of its actions, saying it had cut rates by four percentage points since December 2007. Again, as we've seen, that is true, but with some pauses and fumbling around first.

But it's clear now that we were also approaching the "whatever it takes" zone that global leaders would lay out. Later in March, Carney gave an existential speech, "What Are Banks Really For?"

From here, looking back, knowing that Carney's career would become historic, with him becoming the first foreigner to lead the Bank of England, we should note again that while Canada's extraordinary resilience and sound banking system was vital, we also had a standalone bank regulator, OSFI, and further oversight from the finance department. Carney's actions were bold and effective, but they might not have worked so well if we had the same rot in our financial system as the U.S. and parts of Europe had.

In April, we did indeed enter emergency measures territory.

Effectively zero rates

The April 2009 decision was arguably the most important in the two decades covered in this book.

Firstly, it brought the key rate down to 0.25 percent, and it's never gone lower, even as later, under Governor Poloz the Bank would say you could go to about -0.5 percent and still have the financial system working effectively. Tiff Macklem also affirmed that a negative rate was in the toolkit, but said it would unlikely ever get to that. So Carney set the floor for any future crisis. Even today, policy makers and economists often use the term "effective lower bound" when referring to a 0.25 percent interest rate.

This decision also set down a marker against buying bonds to push interest rates down further on longer-term loans, a policy known as quantitative easing (QE)—Quantitative because the amount of bonds you purchase becomes the measure of how much easing you are doing. While we moved into QE in 2020, this set Canada apart from the U.S., in particular. The Bank also laid down some advance principles for using QE, if it came to that point, signaling that even the use of QE would come with limits to ensure it was effective. This was a good idea, because at the time, there wasn't great confidence that the policy would accomplish very much.

The "conditional commitment" to freeze rates around zero

Third, and most relevant, Carney laid out the extraordinary "conditional commitment," a test of the power of explicit forward guidance. He pledged to hold the interest rate at 0.25 percent until the second quarter of 2010. For investors obsessed with what the Bank of Canada would do at eight decisions a year, this was providing certainty for a quite a long time.

Recall that until around 2000, the best thinking was that you never had to announce any rate move, you just went into the market any day you wanted at 9 a.m., and starting moving things around, because a surprise was supposed to be more effective.

This commitment was a big gamble. What if investors six months later saw a strong rebound coming, pushed up bond yields and openly questioned whether the Bank would break its promise? Would anyone believe the next promise? Even if the Bank called its promise conditional, it was hard to believe that people would see that aspect of it. Put another way, you couldn't really buy into the idea that rates would stay low if you believed in the conditionality of the promise. Conditional love doesn't make for a good marriage.

In the end, Carney didn't quite make it all the way to what you could see as the time he promised, but it was close enough that markets didn't care.

This is a case where the Bank didn't overreact to the weakness, bad as it was. Imagine cutting the rate to zero or starting asset purchases, and then less than a year later, having to unwind?

The Bank said candidly that, even with all this stimulus, there was risk the economy would still suffer even further. Officials saw prices falling 0.8 percent in the third quarter, and projected that it would take two years to return to the two percent target.

Here is the famous phrase: "Conditional on the outlook for inflation, the target overnight rate can be expected to remain at its current level until the end of the second quarter of 2010 in order to achieve the inflation target. The Bank will continue to provide such guidance in its scheduled interest rate announcements as long as the overnight rate is at the effective lower bound."

If you read closely, you will notice it says "until the end of the second quarter of 2010." Remember that!

Avoiding negative interest rates

On paper, the Bank of Canada could have cut interest rates to zero. Other nations embraced negative interest rates. Why didn't the Bank of Canada try this?

Negative interest rates are too difficult to explain to the public with any confidence. Even if the negative rate is a "wholesale" rate that the public will never experience for themselves, you can't get around the message that the world is upside down. For policy makers aiming to stabilize public confidence, this not a good message.

Also, I don't see a compelling example of a major economy getting into these extreme policies and then getting out in short order with a healthy economy. This is what economists have called a "liquidity trap," where low interest rates will never fix a problem of weak demand. If someone could tell me that, as with a regular interest rate cut, the benefits will take "so many months" to go through, and then after that, you can get out with a visible benefit, that might be something. But that's not what we get; we get a semi-permanent policy with no clear conditions for going deeper or getting out. In other words, a morass.

You could also argue that if cutting by two or three percentage points of ordinary rate cuts don't work, why would the extra half a point—going negative—turn things around?

Secondly, given what we learned about hidden weaknesses in financial markets in 2008 globally, on the surface, it seems you are taking a risk that you will break other things in the markets.

After this point, every statement came with an update on how this conditional commitment was doing. In June, the Bank of Canada introduced a new wrinkle to signs of an economic recovery. "In recent weeks, financial conditions and commodity prices have improved significantly, and consumer and business confidence have recovered modestly. If the unprecedentedly rapid rise in the Canadian dollar (which reflects a combination of higher commodity prices and generalized weakness in the U.S. currency) proves persistent, it could fully offset these positive factors."

While the Bank of Canada mostly gave up trying to manage the Canadian dollar's value in global markets after a failed attempt in 1998, it still occasionally suggests this kind of concern with the currency's value. This kind of "jawboning" about the currency is a sign that the Bank sometimes has to "lean against" the currency's exchange rate. These are signs that policy makers really believe the Canadian dollar is potentially interfering with how the broader economy should function.

Green Shoots

By July 2009, we were already hearing the phrase "green shoots" when talking about signs the recovery was coming, and the words "global recession" were being used in the past tense. A long list of positive signs, including consumer confidence, was tempered by a bit more danger from Canada's strong dollar, but the language had improved quite a bit from a few months earlier. So, too early to talk about that conditional commitment yet?

The year's policy meetings would end in December with the Bank saying the domestic economy was now progressing as it had expected, and inflation would get to target by the second half of 2011. Again, by now you could almost hear market renegades saying Carney would have to fold up his conditional commitment early.

This question wasn't trivial. The Fed is still being razzed by investors for its "taper tantrum" when it moved to pare back asset purchases, a somewhat unexpected shift that caused a surge in bond yields and threatened to hurt the U.S. recovery. When Carney got to the U.K., he was also grilled over perceived infidelities in signals to markets and the public.

Indebted consumers as an afterthought

Carney's last speech of the year was "Current Issues in Household Finances," a topic still at the beating heart of our economy today.

Here's an eerie line in the remarks, still relevant today: "the vulnerability of Canadian households to adverse wealth and income shocks has grown in recent years. Aggregate debt levels have risen sharply relative to income. Those debt levels have continued to grow fairly rapidly this year, unusually so for a recession."

It would be nice to know if there is any clear threshold where the Bank of Canada would shift monetary policy to put a check on housing and consumer debt.

Whether or not low interest rates got Canadians drunk on million-dollar mortgages and a reckless housing boom is a very complicated question. But the era of "low-for-long" interest rates was clearly a factor. Governor Poloz sometimes likened this problem to a surgeon doing emergency surgery with side effects, arguing that *not* taking strong action would have been worse. That's for Canadians to judge.

One remarkable thing we learned after 2008-09 was that Canada's ratio of debt to after-tax income would rise above the U.S. level that was recorded before its housing crash. Put another way, a few years ago, household debt in Canada grew bigger than our gross domestic product. Even if all of this is relatively stable, the share of housing and consumer debt in our society is big enough by itself to influence economic growth, employment, and inflation on a scale similar to major industries like manufacturing and natural resource production.

The long-term growth of housing prices from around 2009 to today makes this less of a bubble and more of a long-run trend. It seems clear that the global and metropolitan cities of Canada are on their way to being more like London, Paris, Tokyo, and New York, in that getting a nice condo will require a big investment. Even if there is a housing crash of twenty percent, the price of a home in Vancouver would fall from about 1.1 million dollars to something very many Canadians would still find out of reach. The loss of affordability raises big questions about how people finance their houses, one that is increasingly being asked of governments.

Governments who wish to make it more affordable to buy a house must ask themselves if that is responsible in a healthy economy. More to the point, if the going price is a million dollars, in some ways it's expensive even for very rich families, so making housing more affordable is really about picking out certain types of favoured buyers.

The pandemic also showed a period with no immigration, in which home prices and sales still took off, so it wasn't a classic speculator bubble driven by foreigners. In the end, the jump in housing prices may also be making a generation of Canadians "house poor," which has implications for consumer spending.

CHAPTER EIGHT

Green stalks of 2010

Revisiting the conditional commitment

Getting back to the conditional commitment, the January 2010 meeting had more evidence that things were going well. Global growth was stronger than expected, inflation had turned positive, and core inflation was stronger than expected. While the economy was still dependent on stimulus and the dollar was a drag on exports, was this really a situation that needed emergency support?

While repeating the conditional commitment, Carney was still holding onto the caveat that inflation risks were still tilted a bit to the downside. One clear message from 2008 at the start was that central banks wanted policy support to clearly pull the economy out of the mud. Looking back on this today, such caution has won more justification. Many governments around the world were keen to end fiscal support when the economy was returning to normal, a withdrawal that has since been blamed by some for leading to a long period of weak growth as economies never reached launch speed.

This tension over how fast to pull back on monetary stimulus has loomed large, around 2010 and again in 2020. One big contrast between 2010 and 2020 was the preoccupation in 2010 with getting ahead of inflation before it got out of hand. If it takes a year for an interest rate hike to restrain the economy, that can mean you need to tighten monetary policy before inflation even begins showing up in the numbers.

In 2020, the world had seen "slow-flation" for so long that, according to the Federal Reserve, you needed to overshoot just to prove you could sustain two percent inflation. Bank of Canada officials also spoke often about the mystery of weak inflation pressure. In other words, today, policy makers would rather let the economy run hot and see how much job growth and output can be restored, rather than moving to cut off inflation in advance.

In 2022, we are seeing the impact of the opposite problem, waiting too long to raise interest rates and then tightening very quickly in attempt to catch up. Now the danger is whether these fast rate hikes will in fact slow the economy just as it needs support after stabilizing from the depths of the pandemic lockdowns.

Fuzzy commitment?

In March of 2010, the Bank of Canada affirmed "Conditional on the current outlook for inflation, the target overnight rate can be expected to remain at its current level until the end of the second quarter of 2010 in order to achieve the inflation target." Remember—the end of the second quarter—so that meeting in April is easy money, right?

Here is the Bank of Canada's April 2010 press release headline: "Bank of Canada maintains overnight rate target at 1/4 percent; removes conditional commitment."

That is one meeting before the end of the second quarter, and arguably, they should have held the commitment even at the June meeting. Investors generally said it was close enough, which mainly tells us markets are fickle. In essence, the feeling was that given the strains of the last year, this was a conditional commitment that had worked well enough.

You can see in the statement all the implicit outs the Bank gave itself, stressing that the commitment was conditional, and it had done its job. It also shows how sensitive the Bank was at the time to explain itself on this subject:

"With its conditional commitment introduced in April 2009, the Bank also provided exceptional guidance on the likely path of its target rate."

"This unconventional policy provided considerable additional stimulus during a period of very weak economic conditions and major downside risks to the global and Canadian economies."

"With recent improvements in the economic outlook, the need for such extraordinary policy is now passing, and it is appropriate to begin to lessen the degree of monetary stimulus."

Lifting rates off the floor

The June 1 statement was another opportunity to evaluate whether the commitment was kept.

The headline of the decision was: "Bank of Canada increases overnight rate target to a half percent and re-establishes normal functioning of the overnight market."

This argues that it's a small rate increase, and the announcement came with other moves that were taking things back somewhat to normal. Carney also injected some other stability into all of this, warning us not to expect rates to jump along with the recovery. We went from conditional commitment to a more regular soft forward guidance. "Given the considerable uncertainty surrounding the outlook, any further reduction of monetary stimulus would have to be weighed carefully against domestic and global economic developments."

While one can quibble about whether the promise was fully kept, this must be weighed against emergency action in a very difficult time. The Bank also avoided going further than needed into its unconventional tools, and most importantly, helped foster a recovery from the worst downturn since the Great Depression. There was also a genuine exit strategy that came without markets going haywire.

Plaudits for Carney started coming in. He became Chairman of the Committee on the Global Financial System, a three-year gig. This was a club of central bankers arranged, in part, by the Bank for International Settlements, kind of a central bank for central banks, based in Switzerland. He took over from the Fed's Donald Kohn. This was a big deal for a world that often didn't turn to Canada for financial advice, given the dominant trading floors in New York, Tokyo, Frankfurt, and London. Late that year, Carney would also become Chair of the Financial Stability Board (FSB), a role that G20 leaders signed off on. He also replaced another big name, Mario Draghi of the European Central Bank.

Hiking and serial disappointment

July 2010, Carney raised the overnight interest rate another quarter point to 0.75 percent, and then to one percent in September, another vote of confidence in the building recovery. Sadly, there would not be too many more of those votes, and no more six percent policy rates.

The pause would come in October 2010 as the U.S. recovery was looking weaker, and Canada's, too. Another stumbling block was the emerging Greek debt crisis, where investors balked as that country's budget deficit swelled to fifteen percent of GDP in 2009. This hurt confidence in debt markets across Europe, and even in the mighty euro.

Carney also noted that at some point, the recovery "is expected to shift away from government and household expenditures towards business investment and net exports."

This hope for a business-led expansion would later be dubbed the "serial disappointment" by Stephen Poloz. Even today, Canada appears very wedded to the idea that economic growth will once again be dominated by growing exports to the U.S. and related business investment. This runs against evidence that China and Mexico have taken a good slice of our share of global exports going to the U.S. This may be one reason that Canada's dollar in recent years hasn't made the big headlines that its movements did in the early 2000s. The weaker manufacturers and exporters who were hurt by the currency's strength and volatility have already been squeezed out.

The Bank of Canada signaled that further rate increases would be difficult, even from a level that was staggeringly low: "At this time of transition in the global recovery, with a weaker U.S. outlook, constraints beginning to moderate growth in emerging-market economies, and domestic considerations that are expected to slow consumption and housing activity in Canada, any further reduction in monetary policy stimulus would need to be carefully considered."

The policy rate was still stuck at one percent more than a year after the conditional commitment was erased. This could have been another opportunity to ask why the Bank didn't wait a couple of meetings so that it could keep its promise, given the economy wasn't really ripping off its shackles.

The July 2011 decision blamed slow U.S. growth and European austerity, and disasters that hit Japan in March. Canada's "rotation of demand" was also slower than expected. The Bank also assumed Europe would be able to contain its sovereign debt crisis, "although there are clear risks around this outcome."

This era drove home the idea that globalization had its downside. It was hard to argue that spreading trade and capital flows around the world had distributed risk better and made us financially safer.

The Covid epidemic also raised questions about the physical delivery of goods such as medical supplies and even automobiles across such far-flung networks. In a sense, when you think about today's populist politics, one root of that tree is surely that ordinary people have very tangible and negative ways of judging open trade and investment flows. In Canada, we also saw the pain of auto bailouts and layoffs, and while economists can argue there are bigger benefits from low prices and quality goods from abroad, it's hard to extinguish the anger families and communities feel from seeing job losses and factory closures. How can a government ever make someone who has lost such things whole again?

Amid this turmoil, the Bank and the government in November 2011 again renewed the two percent target. The most common quote I have gathered in the months and years reporting on all these reviews is: "If it ain't broke, don't fix it."

CHAPTER NINE

From Carney to Poloz, and the Longest Pause

As 2012 began, we were getting entrenched in the long interest-rate pause. The January decision noted that we had a lot of economic stimulus, and there was no clue as to any move beyond one percent: "The Bank will continue to monitor carefully economic and financial developments in the Canadian and global economies, together with the evolution of risks, and set monetary policy consistent with achieving the 2 percent inflation target over the medium term.

Central banks always monitor the economy, so there was no clue there. There seemed to be little discomfort with the inflation target, and the risks around it were "roughly balanced," so no clue there either.

Here I should give a shout out to Deputy Governor John Murray. His speech, outlining exactly how the Governing Council comes to a rate decision, from briefings to the final meeting, knocks down some misconceptions about central banking. (See: https://www.bankofcanada.ca/2012/05/monetary-policy-decision-making/)

The Currency and Dutch Disease?

The relative calm of 2012 did have a flashpoint when Carney got into the debate about whether Canada's commodity (especially crude oil) boom was giving us "Dutch Disease." In other words, would the rest of our economy be hollowed out by a surge in commodity prices that lured too much activity into that part of the economy, pushing up our dollar, making exporters uncompetitive, and channeling too much investment and too many workers to boomtowns, and so on. In this era following the auto bailouts, this was a bit touchy. One thing that was clear in global data was that most advanced nations had seen manufacturing fall as a share of employment and GDP for a while, either because of the rise of a service economy or perhaps because of the rise of China and other emerging market economies. Canada was by no means alone in seeing factory employment fade, suggesting our oil boom was not the singular culprit.

Carney spoke in Calgary on Sept. 7 and called higher commodity prices "unambiguously good" for Canada. His fourth paragraph read "While the tidiness of the argument is appealing and making commodities the scape-goat is tempting, the diagnosis is overly simplistic and, in the end, wrong. Canada's economy is much more diverse and much better integrated than the Dutch Disease caricature."

Carney also marshalled the argument that only half of the Canadian dollar's rise was linked to higher commodity prices, while forty percent is linked to a weaker U.S. economy and currency. The stronger dollar would also help firms import equipment to boost their productivity, he said. Hence, leaning into the strong currency wasn't an option, as the Bank would only do such a thing in extreme circumstances, he said.

While all this sounds reasonable, he wound up with another punchy bit: "The logic of Dutch Disease requires that we undo our successes in order to depreciate our currency. Taken to its natural conclusion, this logic dictates that we shut down the oil sands, abandon our resource wealth, have high and variable inflation, run large fiscal deficits, and diminish our financial sector."

[And if you thought Dutch disease was linked to the tulip mania centuries ago, as I did, it was in fact a big natural gas discovery noted by *The Economist* in 1977, according to Carney's footnotes.]

I can't sort out all the arguments here. It's fair to say that times of a weaker dollar, over the time I've watched the economy, never unleashed a manufacturing boom. Nor has a dollar at or above parity, by itself, wiped out manufacturing beyond some of the weaker links. I have seen some evidence that companies adapt to a higher dollar by expanding U.S. operations, avoiding converting the currencies back and forth, and big firms who need to borrow in U.S. dollars making sure they have financial contracts that guard against the risk of currency fluctuations as they pay back the loans.

What's been more striking in recent years is how stable the Canadian dollar has been amid all the global turmoil and swings in commodity prices. The dollar is no longer grabbing front-page headlines. It's possible some of the optimism about an Alberta oil boom has swung to concern about a shift to green energy, and it's possible there's less upside for Canadian exports after losing market share in the U.S.

Hello Governor: Carney crosses the pond into history

On November 26, 2012, came the announcement that Carney would leave for the Bank of England, staying in Canada until next June to help the transition to a new Governor to replace him.

As a journalist, I am skeptical about using the word "unprecedented," but this event was close. I would point out the first Governor of the Bank of Canada, Graham Towers. According to *Graham Towers and His Times* by Douglas Fullerton, Towers, after leaving the Bank, joined the board of General Motors in 1958, and later turned down a larger role. When the motto "As goes General Motors, so goes the U.S." mattered, this was probably on par with Carney's big move. Towers also turned down "a sporty new Toronado" in favour of a Buick, more in his modest style. Towers also quietly helped Canada with the auto pact with the U.S. in the 1960s, arguably the most influential trade deal Canada ever signed.

It's more than fair to say that Carney's new appointment was historic for the U.K., and for Canada. The Bank of England dates back to 1694, and had never been led by a foreigner.

There were very few precedents anywhere in central banking for such a switch. And of course, it's unusual for a former British colony like Canada to suddenly lead a major institution of the mother country. Questions about London traders and how loosely they were regulated before the crash seemed to have played a role in the desire for outside supervision.

Again, this was an almost total surprise to most financial reporters, who had perhaps heard rumours but they didn't seem to go that far. On that day, this intrepid reporter was out Christmas shopping with a newborn, and didn't notice the appointment until watching the end of a supper-hour newscast.

Carney's appointment was a proud moment for Canada, and frankly, well deserved. I found it a little frustrating how officials from nations who had made grievous errors in oversight sought to regain their place at the top of global financial trading flows, protected their exchanges and banks from foreign competition, and remained willing to continue "light touch" regulation. Carney's appointment was one sign the virtue Canada had shown was being recognized. Canada should have been more vocal in advocating to build a safer financial system after the crisis had passed, and not letting some very large economies forget the pain they helped spread around the world.

Carney, in December 2012, gave a speech looking back at his conditional commitment, signaling that it should remain deep in the toolkit. "Forward guidance of policy is best used sparingly in normal times. In extraordinary times, however, conditional guidance can be used to resolve time inconsistencies and achieve a better path for the economy."

One thing I noticed around this time was that investors, from this point on, called almost anything that moved "forward guidance." So even a clear exit strategy may not, in practice, lead to a clear exit. This development made it harder to cover monetary policy because investors and policy makers were simply not on the same page anymore when describing the economy.

What is perhaps shocking in this Carney speech, but became more shocking later under Poloz, was that Carney went into a lengthy chat about something obvious. Investors should do their own homework and understand, not just central bank code words, Carney argued, but economic forces that might swing things around and lead to a policy change.

"Without this understanding, market participants may be even less able to form efficient expectations over time, thus increasing their reliance on explicit guidance from the central bank. Ultimately, the risk is that markets turn into an echo chamber, to the benefit of no one."

And later, "Actual policy will always respond to the economic and financial outlook as it evolves. Market expectations of policy should do the same, reflecting differences in perspectives amid a common understanding of our objective."

While policy makers sometimes seem to grumble when markets make up their own mind and force the central bank's hand somewhat, they like even less the idea of being responsible for bad bets that investors make and suggestions the Bank of Canada led them astray.

Poloz comes on board, analogies aplenty

With Carney leaving, the government and the Bank's board took until May to announce that Stephen Poloz would be the next Governor, effective June 3, again raising the question about the Senior Deputy not getting the job.

Poloz had been chief economist and CEO at Export Development Canada, and I had attended couple of his presentations. I had seen some of his wilder, by economic standards, slideshow presentations, which included references to superheroes. I was fully prepared for all the future references to Star Trek, the recovery from the financial crisis being like a pot of spaghetti sauce, and lost sailors trying to get home again. This was all fine, and, I thought, very welcome in making complicated messages about the economy clearer to the public, which was the whole point. To me, it takes a very smart person to put something across in a way that sounds too simple. Poloz was clearly full value for his PhD from Western, the university that developed so many of the Bank of Canada's top minds. I don't think the Conservatives at the time minded at all that Poloz was in some ways more ordinary and low-key than Carney had been. Governors somehow seem to fit the times, and Poloz was a fine Governor for an era in which we wanted to put turmoil and crisis in the rear-view mirror.

Poloz also did some strong things such as taking the emphasis away from overly precise economic forecasts that staff produced. (So, for example, did it really matter if growth was 3.3 percent next year or 3.1 percent, or was it easier to say "just over 3 percent" or "about three and a quarter percent." And I would argue that for 99.9 percent of Canadians, the better answer is the round number.) Poloz also, with some success, got across the message that economic models are not the gospel that most economists let the public think they are. Poloz was candid in saying that models are tools, and judgment must prevail in policy decisions. Again, for investors who disliked the feeling of surprise when interest rates were cut in 2015, it would have been wise to have seen his perspective.

There is a major problem with relying on judgment. If you are wrong, you can't put the blame on the regular precise economic tools the Bank uses to monitor the economy. Another problem is consistency. Poloz, like other Governors, tended to move back and forth between judgment and relying on economic data. However, Poloz was very familiar with these issues since he had been at the Bank earlier in his career, rising to chief of the research department in 1992. While he may have looked like an outsider at first, it wasn't his first time at the central bank.

Canada's fiscal resilience

Carney's last speech in late May pulled together why Canada avoided the fate of other advanced nations. "Responsible fiscal policy, sound monetary policy, a resilient financial system, and a monetary union that works." Canada did indeed, after the Global Financial Crisis, draw some favourable reviews from abroad for having an economic model that worked. This was a big change from not so long ago.

In the 1990s, Canada was seen by *The Wall Street Journal* as having a "northern peso," and credit rating agencies were cutting our grades while global investors fled. That great scare pushed Paul Martin into his "hell or high water" budgets, which painfully balanced the books, stabilized a shaky pension system, and gave the Bank of Canada inflation targets. The government famously also blocked bank mega-mergers and kept our small and oligopolistic banks from merging. (Some have noted that this may have protected Canada from potential takeovers from U.S. banks that could have pulled us into the 2008 crisis more directly.)

Along with our resilient financial system, Canada had a more unified monetary and fiscal system. That contrasted with the Eurozone, founded with the basic premise of blunting the possibility of another world war while uniting an impressive trade bloc under a single currency that was supposed to rival the U.S. dollar for global primacy.

To keep it together, there was also supposed to be unity on meeting fiscal targets, to keep each member state in the zone moving at around the same pace. Over time, the lack of unity led to intense pressure in Greece and Ireland, for example, and they didn't have traditional escape hatch of a currency devaluation. Beyond national borders, investors also worried about whether other nations who held large amount of debt from weaker economies would end up damaged as well. Canada's advantage is that it's fairly clear to bondholders that a provincial government in big trouble is essentially guaranteed by the federal government, and that fiscal transfers to provinces are big enough to ward off any major fragmentation. All provinces face strong political peer pressure to deliver comparable services at comparable rates of spending and taxation.

Carney also cited figures suggesting that Canada's labour mobility between provinces was about four times greater than labour mobility within Europe. And the continent's banking system is also fragmented, unlike Canada's.

At the end of May, Carney left office with a one percent policy rate. Carney also left in place a soft bias (this was now the word in vogue among markets) to raise rates, again on the disappointing premise that investment and exports would boost the recovery, while household debt ratios would stabilize. "The considerable monetary policy stimulus currently in place will likely remain appropriate for a period of time, after which some modest withdrawal will likely be required."

It felt unsatisfying that the Bank of Canada left interest rates so low, hoping business spending and investment would lead the economy, while downplaying the risks of a consumer debt buildup. Monetary policy has limits. This perhaps was the classic trap of "pushing on a string," where low interest rates are ineffective in a world where companies had little incentive to ramp up investment.

Similarly, in recent years, there has been a global push from governments to take back some of the major tax cuts offered to corporations on the premise it would lead to more jobs and investment. One troubling feature of Canada's economy is that even after major corporate tax cuts, companies still spend far less on worker training and equipment than American competitors.

Looking from the Carney era to today, the issues of heavy consumer debts and stretched housing markets have only intensified as a negative side effect of low interest rates.

Serial disappointment

Stephen Poloz's debut as Governor came on June 6, 2013, three days after officially taking over, with perhaps the most dreaded of tasks, a parliamentary hearing. Prepare all the facts you want: typical hearings have a segment of partisan questions asking the Governor of an independent central bank to weigh in on whether the Liberal or Conservative plan to do "whatever" is a great idea. Worse, they will blindside you with an obscure part of something you are responsible for, but with a question that's either way too precise for an oral answer or too vague to deliver something useful.

Poloz inherited Carney's bias to raise rates, and in early market reviews, was seen as favouring a weak dollar (without much real evidence). Poloz's testimony likened the recovery from the global financial crisis as a postwar rebuild, a very sharp description for an economy that avoided a banking or housing collapse. "We need to see the reconstruction of Canada's economic potential, and a return to self-sustaining, self-generating growth."

We could skip over the seven-year term under Poloz and just say that this goal was never reached, for a variety of reasons both within and outside of Canada's control. Poloz said a few times near the end of his term that we had basically gotten "home" again, but it was never that clear.

Later that June marked his first speech somewhere in the blurry suburbs west of Toronto. (Was I in Burlington or Oakville?) Poloz noted that, beyond a typical recession, in which firms may cut back production and jobs, there was evidence that smaller exporters had closed for good, and it would take some work to get that production back. Exports were one hundred billion dollars below where they might have been at that point in a normal economic cycle.

He also provided a look at the strength of the housing market and, as with exports and investment, it was remarkable that these issues would still be on the table at the end of his term and beyond: "The Bank has been careful to remind people that interest rates will rise at some point. We have urged homeowners and other borrowers to do the arithmetic to ensure that they will be able to manage their debts at more normal interest rates. I am confident that this is exactly what people are doing."

That was not what people were doing. Provincial and federal governments would later see prices rising in some hot markets at a thirty percent year-over-year pace, and put the hammer down with rules aimed at speculators and foreign buyers. Later, a stress test, would be added for borrowers of new mortgages. Governments are still trying to figure out how else they can clamp down on speculation today.

The big news as 2013 wound down was Tiff Macklem saying he would leave as the Bank of Canada's Senior Deputy in May to run the University of Toronto's Rotman business school. This was well before the end of his seven-year term, which only began in July 2010. This created some shock and disappointment among staff. So did the retirement of John Murray later that month. With Carney's departure, this meant that quite a bit of brainpower and experience was leaving the firm.

Carolyn Wilkins took over as Senior Deputy in May 2014, for a seven-year term. She was given a more prominent role by Poloz than past senior deputies had been given. A few times, she ended up reading the opening statement at the press conference following a rate decision.

Wilkins would also leave early after Tiff Mackem returned as Governor. The bank needed a woman in the top ranks. When she left, the panel was exclusively left with men, and no visible minorities. At a time when the government was actively talking about a major economic crisis and the need to understand how it was hurting women and minorities, this was doubly bad. While the Bank isn't political, in Ottawa culture, it was also out of tune with a gender-balanced federal cabinet and some more prominent opposition critic roles being given to women.

CHAPTER TEN

The Longest Pause, Serial disappointment, and Poloz Gives Investors Fair Warning

Markets ignore an essential Poloz paper

Back to our long freeze on interest rates. By mid-2014, the one percent overnight rate had been in place for so long the bank was reduced to giving speeches titled "Monetary Policy and the Underwhelming Recovery," and "Are We There Yet? The United States and Canada After the Global Financial Crisis."

Poloz had the time to write a research paper, one I was surprised many investors clearly never read. They would pay dearly for that mistake. Governors of central banks don't have much time to write these kinds of papers, so when they do, they bear reading. The bank didn't hide the paper, either; they put out a press release about it.

The title screamed essential reading for investors and academic economists: "Integrating Uncertainty and Monetary Policy-Making: A Practitioner's Perspective."

The press release offered another big clue, stating "risk management" must be how policy makers look at the economy. In other words, rather than be bound by reading the tea leaves from the flow of economic data, it's best to keep an eye on the biggest things that can go right and wrong and act accordingly. If there are risks that inflation could be faster or slower than expected, but the downside scenario is stubbornly low prices that take years to correct, you might set policy to deal with the bigger risk.

More importantly for markets, Poloz laid out a case that "forward guidance" is only a big help when interest rates are close to zero. (In that case, guidance lets markets know in an economic downturn that rates will be as low as possible for a while, helping pull down the cost of borrowing for longer-term loan—more than a central bank could normally engineer.)

Otherwise, Poloz wrote that forward guidance can encourage markets to make relentless "one-way" bets based on the guidance policy makers have fed them. Poloz suggested it's the job of investors to assess the risks around monetary policy themselves, not have it handed it to them by policymakers. Without this, the financial markets can become even more volatile when they think the central bank will pull its guidance, or as Poloz said, "the lunch may not be entirely free."

Markets may also need "repeated doses of insurance" that the conditions to keep the guidance in place, such as weak inflation and so on, are still in place. He made this even more visceral: "In short, forward guidance can become addictive for markets if it is overly precise or heavily weighted with caveats."

"Forward guidance should be seen as a useful tool in the central banker's kit, but one that should be reserved primarily for use at the zero lower bound, as a form of additional insurance that the economy will return to equilibrium," Poloz argued.

In other public comments, Poloz also signaled that he saw every interest-rate announcement as a "clean sheet." There was little need to carry over the language policy makers had used a few months earlier to describe the economy into the next decision statement. This is radically different from the U.S. Federal Reserve statements; most of the time the rate decisions are templates, and they may only change a few sentences or even a few words if the economy is on the same path. Even major changes of the Fed's direction can be summed up in one or two key changes.

Of course, even the Bank sometimes changes expectations with just a few words. Poloz's stance was a gauntlet thrown down to markets. Figure out your own risks, your own forecasts. I am prepared to make big changes if I see a significant risk, maybe even ones that don't show up in standard economic models.

Of course, he closed on an analogy. "We know that the sailors of yore who drifted into the southern hemisphere coped. They adapted to the new constellations and found their way—as will we."

Looking back at the way markets complained about his surprise interest rate cut, I also wonder if the Bank could have quietly reached out to market players to tell them this was serious. Maybe they did.

Highly paid investors fail to read Governor Poloz

This was also a fascinating case of the individuality of each Governor. When Stephen Poloz became Governor after Carney, markets wondered if he could handle markets like Carney of Goldman Sachs, or if because Poloz came from the government export bank, he would allow a weak dollar.

So when Poloz wrote a paper about financial markets, I duly wrote up the story, told many people I spoke to how rare this was, and noted that at some point, we should expect a surprise rate move.

I thought all the highly paid traders would have received Poloz's message, too. When Poloz cut rates in 2015 with no clear advance signaling, some investors were outraged. They accused the Bank of going dark over the Christmas holiday when they should have been rousing us from sugarplum dreams to warn of a quarter point rate cut.

Late that year, everyone, including me, had somehow missed this critical fact: the price of crude oil, which around this time had overtaken automobiles as Canada's top export, had fallen by half in world markets. This was even harder on Alberta's oilsands, deposits that are more expensive to turn into crude oil than Texas crude is.

So, the Canadian economy, classically dependent on commodities and commodity prices, saw a massive plunge in its staple product. And this slide had been going on for months, not weeks.

You didn't have to be Steve Poloz, former chief economist at Export Development Canada, to figure out what this meant for the economy. So when Governor Poloz cut the rate a quarter point in January, and again a bit later, it was exactly the right thing to do. It made our downturn milder than it could have been, and was also an early wakeup call to the public.

A year or two later, when Poloz was vindicated for what turned out to be his prescient call, he got less praise and more grumbling that he still should have warned us. Some investors never really forgave or trusted him after that. Maybe blaming Poloz as unreliable was easier than telling their clients they missed the obvious.

Poloz puts theory into practice

At the end of 2014, we seemed to slip back into more regular monetary policy, but also a stance that touched on the idea of "risk management." On December 3, 2014, the Bank held rates at one percent, which took few by surprise because by that time the economy was on the mend.

The decision mentioned that inflation had risen more than expected, mainly on temporary factors, but that "underlying inflation" has also moved up. There were also references to a stronger U.S. economy, and that "oil prices have continued to fall." Canada was seeing "signs of a broadening recovery," although lower oil and commodity prices would "weigh" on the economy.

Then we got this: "While inflation is at a higher starting point relative to the October MPR, weaker oil prices pose an important downside risk to the inflation profile. This is tempered by a stronger U.S. economy, Canadian dollar depreciation, and recent federal fiscal measures. Household imbalances, meanwhile, present a significant risk to financial stability. Overall, the balance of risks remains within the zone for which the current stance of monetary policy is appropriate and therefore the target for the overnight rate remains at 1 percent."

Oil prices posing an important downside risk was a big statement, but it was couched against other positives, giving a sense of the Bank's usual balance. Either way, markets were not betting on a rate cut after this decision.

One last thing to note. The Bank mentioned that while the production side of the economy seemed tighter, "the labour market continues to indicate significant slack." One thing that makes Canada's central bank unique, and perhaps more effective, is the fact it has a single goal of keeping inflation at two percent, and no significant mandate to boost employment.

The Federal Reserve's mandate from Congress has a dual goal of price stability and maximum employment. For the Bank of Canada, there was little idea of trying to run the economy "hot" to create more jobs. This focus is one reason the Bank of Canada has done better than some of its peers in controlling inflation. But in this case, you could not list the weak job market as a major signal that interest rates might be cut.

But maybe he didn't give fair warning?

Poloz gave his yearend speech on Dec. 11 in New York, and it was tailored to financial market folks. The speech lacked the traditional section about Canada's economic outlook, not even a bare repetition of the recent interest-rate decision.

The word "oil" wasn't in the speech either.

There was still one more chance to warn markets about the rate cut that would break the long pause (at one percent) in January 2015. That was a Jan. 13 speech by Deputy Tim Lane in Wisconsin. (Yes, Wisconsin.)

Suffice it to say, no one thought enough about the title "Drilling Down - Understanding Oil Prices and Their Economic Impact." Lane noted the recent big drop in oil prices and how important oil was to Canada's economy, but the comments read like statements of stylized facts to jog the audience's memory. Lane also highlighted that the rise of China suggested a long-term demand for oil.

Lane said, "the most recent Bank of Canada projections show a global growth rate of 3½ percent this year and next, compared with 3 percent last year." This was hardly a signal of a dangerous global slump.

Even in the discussion about lower oil prices, he suggested that it would take further weakness before firms would take existing production offline, a force that might just simply bring demand and supply into balance. He also made a few mentions of price "overshoots": a standard term to economists. The phrase describes how financial markets move faster and harder in response to new information than long-term fundamentals would suggest.

"Putting all the pieces together, we conclude that there are two-sided risks around current oil prices: sizable short-run movements in either direction are quite possible."

He later reverted to the thoughts of the last rate decision. Yes, lower oil prices may be a problem, but there's wider strength, too.

> "Signs of a broadening recovery have been emerging during the past year. Stronger U.S. growth and a weaker Canadian dollar have boosted non-energy exports. Investment spending and job creation have also begun to pick up, although significant slack remains in the labour market. In that context, we see important risks to Canada's economic outlook stemming from the recent decline in the price of oil and other commodities. As a net oil exporter, Canada will be affected by the lower prices, operating through several channels."

So again, the oil weakness is within a broader context. For a central bank that doesn't wish to react to a single industry's problems, this sounds like business as usual. Then it flips back to this:

> "Despite the mitigating factors I enumerated, lower oil prices are likely, on the whole, to be bad for Canada. Estimating the magnitude of that overall impact requires carefully analyzing the interplay between the various effects as they work through the economy. That is what we are doing as we prepare next week's forecast."

> For the Bank of Canada, there are two main takeaways from the drop in oil prices. First, we will look through its immediate and temporary negative effect on total consumer price inflation. Second, we will closely monitor its broader impacts on growth and the delay it may cause to the economy's return to its production potential. We will also watch for any impacts on the rotation of demand that we have begun to witness."

On the surface, we seem to be getting into somewhat contradictory messages. The speech ended in a similar way:

> "These developments are among the most important that the Bank of Canada takes into account in making monetary

policy. We will continue to work to bring the Canadian economy back to its potential and return inflation sustainably to our 2 percent target. However things play out, we have the tools to respond."

In hindsight, it's surprising to see a central bank that targets inflation, and historically has shunned focusing on one industry, to signal misgivings about the energy sector. The Bank of Canada doesn't even project crude oil prices, they just take the recent price as given and uses that as its assumed future price in its economic forecasts.

There was also no warning here of massive Canadian economic weakness outside of the oil patch and perhaps overall business investment, which had already been weak for several years.

To recap, on Dec. 3 when the last rate decision was made, officials said the economy was "showing signs of a broadening recovery," and in October the Bank saw 2015 GDP growth at 2.4 percent.

On Dec. 11, Poloz made no mention of a significant risk to the economy in his New York speech.

On Jan. 12, the Bank released a quarterly survey of business expectations that showed strengthening demand among manufacturers and exporters, and weakness in energy.

On Jan. 13, the Bank presented a mix of ideas about an economy with hot spots and cold spots.

This is probably why many saw what came next as a surprise, especially since few were doing their own math on what tumbling crude oil prices would mean for Canada.

CHAPTER 11: The oil slump cut of 2015

What experts should have seen coming after oil prices plunged

Shortly after the Lane speech, the Bank of Canada cut interest rates. And suddenly, one industry was identified as being able to tip the whole economy in the Bank's decision statement: "This decision is in response to the recent sharp drop in oil prices, which will be negative for growth and underlying inflation in Canada."

"Canada's weaker terms of trade will have an adverse impact on incomes and wealth, reducing domestic demand growth."

The Bank also said that the economy would still return to full capacity just "a little later than was expected in October."

Poloz suggested this was just a good insurance policy against weakness. "The Bank's policy action is intended to provide insurance against these risks, support the sectoral adjustment needed to strengthen investment and growth, and bring the Canadian economy back to full capacity, and inflation to target, within the projection horizon."

Of course, he turned out to be almost magically correct in the idea the economy was headed towards a recession and he could get in front of it. Later, when he was asked to take some credit for it, he humbly said it was the Bank staff that figured this puzzle out. Even so, only Poloz would have worn the goat horns if the projection turned out wrong. Whether he acted strictly on data, on his newish mantra of avoiding forward guidance, on his judgment, or maybe some panicked CEOs phoning from Calgary, it wasn't clear.

But it probably felt good to be the smartest person in the room, even though it took the rest of us a long time to figure it out.

The shout followed by a whisper

It didn't help the Bank's argument that policy makers followed up the January interest-rate cut with a pause in March, which suggested the dire outcome was perhaps a false alarm.

This line was not going to calm markets either:

> "The Bank continues to expect that most of the negative impact from lower oil prices will appear in the first half of 2015, although it may be even more front-loaded than projected in January. Nevertheless, data for 2014 as a whole suggest the anticipated rotation into stronger growth in non-energy exports and investment is well underway."

Again in April, there was no rate cut, even as the Bank said inflation was at one percent, the very bottom of its tolerance band. This seemed out of step with a Bank that was supposed to keep inflation at two percent.

You could argue that the Bank jumped the gun on a very short-term dislocation, took the market by surprise, and needlessly spooked everyone. Would it have been better to just signal a cut in January, then cut in March when there was more evidence of a slump?

The Bank also signaled clearly that it might move to the sidelines too: "Risks to the outlook for inflation are now roughly balanced and risks to financial stability appear to be evolving as expected. The Bank judges that the current degree of monetary policy stimulus remains appropriate and therefore is maintaining the target for the overnight rate at 3/4 percent."

In May, Poloz gave a speech saying the economy was finding its way home again, then held the rate.

The whisper followed by a rate cut

It was a bit surprising that in July, Poloz was cutting again to 0.5 percent. Now the bank was highlighting that inflation had fallen to one percent, something it had brushed off not that long ago.

The Bank now saw much more weakness in exports and investment, the things Poloz said in May would lead the economy home. And now there were downside risks to inflation. The growth markdown was stark, from 1.9 percent to 1.1 percent for 2015, about as big a drop as I can remember. While consumer spending rose 1.2 percentage points, business investment fell 0.9 percent.

The Bank didn't really give any guidance on what would happen next. In the end, we were in for another long pause as we waited for the business rebound.

Looking back on this, while it's fair to say that investors and smart reporters like me should have figured out that the economy was heading for the rocks and the Bank would cut rates, the messages around the risks and what the Bank was doing were unclear. That could be a reflection of actual uncertainty in the economy, or in the Bank's struggle to find the right story to tell the public.

While Poloz sought to move away from "forward guidance," it remained a headache to deal with repeated arguments from my editors and clients that the Bank was or wasn't giving clues in its language, or did or did not have a bias to raise or lower rates. Once markets believed that such a hidden message was in the report, the perception was very hard to shake off.

Housing afterthoughts

Let's take stock of Canada's housing boom with Governor Poloz's October 2015 speech, "Integrating Financial Stability into Monetary Policy." By this time, the housing market was clearly heating up, and the bank was cutting interest rates back to record lows. It was a fair question to ask whether in fact the idea of risk management was chasing the wrong kind of risk, and underplaying the dangers in the housing market and consumer debts.

The Bank of Canada has often said it's not the lead mover on financial stability. We have the finance minister; the federal bank regulator, OSFI; and provincial and local governments who can regulate the housing market. Above all, consumers and lenders are responsible for their own private decisions.

Experts and other central banks have rightly asked whether you can really deflate a dot-com stock market boom or bond market excess just by raising interest rates.

Still, when it comes to housing, which is so fundamental to real people, and so closely linked to interest rates, it merits a closer look, especially after the pain seen in the U.S. With housing markets booming, Poloz offered this: "The Bank of Canada's view is that monetary policy should be the last line of defence against threats to financial stability, behind the joint responsibility of borrowers and lenders, appropriate regulatory oversight within the financial sector, and sound macroprudential policies."

Poloz also reiterated that the interest-rate cuts of recent years were designed to boost parts of the economy that would respond, including housing. This was fundamental to bringing the economy to its full potential and keeping inflation stable around two percent. To me, this was still an era where the dangers were rising, and the Bank and other folks in charge were shrugging, or waiting to see who would act first. Mostly international investors were betting on a housing crash that would damage smaller lenders and even big banks. It wasn't comfortable to be reporting on. Poloz also argued that "macroprudential" policies could work. This is a fairly loose term, meaning either more regulations, or perhaps other policies that could kick in when things got hot.

Poloz also framed any monetary response as more of an indirect effort to "lean" against a boom, rather than standing on the railway tracks. "I'm defining leaning as choosing a different path for interest rates than would be optimal for the inflation target in order to mitigate risks to financial stability. This could mean, for example, accepting a significant delay in getting inflation back to target so as not to exacerbate financial vulnerabilities along the way."

We should indeed appreciate that it was a practical impossibility in the mid-2000s to hike up interest rates just to stave off a housing bubble that in fact never materialized. The dollar would have shot up in any part of the cycle in which oil prices were rising, likely enough to derail the fragile recovery in the wider economy. Did anyone really want to see another recession or near recession to fight a phantom menace?

Another sign that the boom wasn't caused by foreign speculators was seen in 2020. Immigration was shut off by the pandemic and housing surged even more. The boom spread from the predictable hotspots of Vancouver and Toronto to rural Quebec, Ontario's cottage country, Saskatchewan, and Nova Scotia.

As we left 2015, interest rates were still on hold. This era raised the question: if the Bank cut rates as a risk management or insurance policy to avoid a recession, and we avoided it, should we not reset back to where we were before?

CHAPTER TWELVE

Getting rates off the floor for a while

Two paths for monetary policy: Risk Management versus Data Dependency

By June 2016, Poloz gave a speech saying "Canadian economy making progress." But still no rate increase. In September, it was, "Living with Lower for Longer." But that still doesn't explain the risk management rationale around why the Bank didn't take back one or both of its rate cuts. Surely the housing market posed some risk and the risk of a second significant economic slump had faded. In December 2016, nearly two years after the first interest-rate cut to head off an oil slump, the rates were held again. The assessment then was more weakness in business activity, and significant slack in the economy.

Being back at near-zero interest rates so long after the 2008 crisis was a huge disappointment. We had survived the global banking crash, but failed to expand our global economic presence or become more innovative, while other nations were in trouble. And Alberta folks who printed bumper stickers in the 1970s reminding them never to piss away another oil boom were soon going to be feeling déjà vu.

It would take another half year, until July 2017, to get interest rates off the mat.

In May, while not making an explicit statement, the Bank said that the oil shock had largely passed, a big clue that rates could rise again.

The July statement moved the rate a quarter point to 0.75 percent, affirmed that the oil shock was no longer the dominant story, and said households were driving growth and moving the economy towards its potential. "Future adjustments to the target for the overnight rate will be guided by incoming data as they inform the Bank's inflation outlook, keeping in mind continued uncertainty and financial system vulnerabilities."

This outlook wasn't suggesting much more than maybe getting rates back to where they were before 2015, a humble one percent. That mark was reached at the next rate meeting in September, and Poloz doused expectations for much more.

"Future monetary policy decisions are not predetermined and will be guided by incoming economic data and financial market developments as they inform the outlook for inflation. Particular focus will be given to the evolution of the economy's potential, and to labour market conditions. Furthermore, given elevated household indebtedness, close attention will be paid to the sensitivity of the economy to higher interest rates."

One sign that things were finally getting back to normal from the financial crisis was a statement that you could tie policy changes to regular economic data again, instead of looking for dangerous downside risks. The danger emerging was that so much household debt had built up under easy monetary policy that raising interest rates could deal the economy a major blow. Low interest rates had now become their own danger to the economic recovery. This is quite a turnaround of the maxim about monetary policy that a central bank's job is to take the punchbowl away before the party gets out of hand.

Re-litigating the 2015 rate cuts

The shift away from "risk management" to "data dependence" was made clear in a subsequent Poloz speech. The Governor hammered home why he had cut rates in 2015. The length of this discussion showed that this was still a touchy subject:

> The roughly 50 percent drop in oil prices during 2014 represented a cut of roughly $60 billion per year in export revenue for oil producers. Some of the impacts of this cut were immediately obvious and predictable [...]. However, the BOS (Business Outlook Survey) taken late in 2014, together with additional discussions we had with energy companies, revealed warning signs that went well beyond the decline in business investment. For example, companies in this region told us that they were being flooded by résumés of workers returning from Alberta. Service firms, such as hotel and trucking companies, told us about bookings being suddenly cancelled. Energy-service companies told us that previously signed contracts for construction and exploration work were being renegotiated, or even terminated.

> So, well before the shock started to show up in the statistics, we could see that it would have a significant negative effect on the Canadian economy and the outlook for inflation. This was crucial to our decision to lower interest rates in January 2015. And, as companies cut their investment intentions further, we lowered interest rates again the following July.

> To be clear, our economic models correctly predicted that the collapse in oil prices would be a serious blow. Specifically, our main policy model gave us invaluable insights into how the shock would affect the economy and how the subsequent adjustments would unfold. But the fact that everything we were hearing was supporting these insights increased our confidence that cutting rates was the right course of action.

This is a nice illustration of how economic policy making is a mix of sophisticated economic analysis and what central bankers learn from the business community and the public.

The year 2017 ended with the key interest rate at one percent, mirroring the bottom of the Bank's one percent to three percent target band for inflation. That is a benchmark of how much life support the economy needed almost a decade after the U.S. banking collapse.

The X-factor in policymaking:
Governors hear things we don't

Governor Poloz often spoke about how monetary policy required much judgment, not just adding up different financial statistics. To him, this meant the Bank of Canada's more anecdotal Business Outlook Survey and his own meetings with executives from companies large and small. When looking back at why decisions went in a surprising way, it's always a good idea to pencil in the idea that Governors hear things we won't.

Journalists, members of the public, and investors can scrutinize publicly available economic reports, and the Bank of Canada's own economists may know up to the last minute what the latest internal projections suggest be done. But in the end, Bank of Canada Governors are at Group of Seven and Group of Twenty meetings, and can tap the head of the Federal Reserve or the European Central Bank on the shoulder to privately ask what's really going on. Governors can also get all the secret briefings and the best gossip, and arrange meetings with oil-patch CEOs that we will never hear about. And of course, they speak with the Finance Minister every few weeks and often also meet provincial Premiers and Finance Ministers.

One problem with both risk management and data dependency is that both come with a lot of selectivity. The Bank of Canada can pick and choose its list of risks, or its key economic data. Policy makers can also change the emphasis on these items or walk away from them. This is another reason that the Bank's inflation target is powerful: no matter what else they talk about, they have to meet the goal of keeping the inflation rate around two percent.

We do get a peek into the Bank's intelligence gathering from the quarterly Business Outlook Survey, often released a week or so before an interest-rate meeting. Officials interview about a hundred firms, and they turn what they learn into precise measures of inflation, investment, and hiring plans. Yet that sample size is too small to be statistically significant. In the end, people who watch the bank know the survey's main value is in the ad hoc commentary that officials run alongside it. Careful readers can see whether or not the summary commentary of the report lines up with the numbers, or if there is a positive or negative spin that might show up in the next rate move.

One quirk in the survey has been the questions around firms' inflation expectations. There have been times when the numbers show a move away from the Bank's target, but officials tend to keep writing in that inflation is "well anchored." This was especially the case in late 2021 when inflation was taking off. Officials made a distinction between shorter-term expectations that were elevated, and longer-term expectations that were more in line with the Bank's target.

Another economic statistic that was misleading in 2021 was the "core inflation" measures the Bank of Canada used. These three core rates sought to strip out consumer prices that are volatile; this blurs the actual trend. A few years ago, the Bank created these core measures and moved away from how some other nations define core inflation, measures that excluded mostly food and energy. The core measures were stable all right, to a fault. In 2020, the biggest economic crisis since the 1930s, none of the Bank's three "core" measures of inflation plunged towards zero. Headline inflation, meanwhile, slipped into negative territory, very briefly. When the economy rebounded and inflation snapped back, I noticed that hardly anyone pointed to the core measures as an early warning indicator about the danger of calling inflation "transitory." The core measures did eventually climb, but much too late to be helpful. (In late 2022, the Bank said it was backing away from the "Common" core measure of CPI, following complaints that revisions showing a rise in inflation came too late to be useful.)

Journalists may ask better questions, but audiences can get better answers

On a happier note, sometimes the Bank gives the people exactly what they want. At audience question-and-answer sessions following public speeches, people often aske: "What keeps you up at night?" Poloz rounded out 2017 with a speech, "Three Things Keeping Me Awake at Night," and it was a nice moment. Quite often, an earnest question from a real person gets a better answer than "hardballs" from journalists.

My own approach to asking questions is to ask something neutral and hope for a longer answer. Officials normally know what hot topics are out there, so a long-winded question just provides more potential for an evasive answer. Other times, reporters ask questions aiming to address something investors want more clarity on. Sometimes you do have to throw hard questions in, mostly because it's clear that there is an issue that is being downplayed or an argument that doesn't make sense. In that case, it's best not to apologize or hesitate, just ask the hard question.

Sometimes I prepare questions well in advance, and they fall through on the day of. Worse, someone asks your two best questions just before you are due to put one in at a press conference. And sometimes, you can't think of good question until the last minute and you just go for it. Those have genuinely been some of my best questions, though at the time it's a bit of a gamble. The ones that you find sudden inspiration for sometimes are in fact just mediocre. The other problem is that some decisions invite a lot of good questions, but other decisions are fairly straightforward, so you have to dig deep into your question list.

So, the three things that kept Poloz up at night: cyber threats, household debt, (and now he was saying these imbalances would be in place for a long time), and third, "The Tough Job Market for Young People."

Full disclosure on that last one about youth: I once ran a series of articles with the catchy shorthand of "basement kids," on the suggestion that unemployed young people who may be living with their parents should consider unpaid volunteer work to boost their prospects. This gained angry reaction from student and union groups, and later from politicians, that was worth following. I found some of the reaction to these comments surprising, since they were more in the line of grandfatherly advice than a diatribe. Beneath the surface, the issue of unpaid internships had become even worse since I finished school. It was a case perhaps where central banks, valuing their independence in monetary policy, should be mindful about how far they can go diagnosing social problems. Talking about what young adults should do to get a job is perhaps a bridge too far coming central bankers who are often financially quite comfortable.

New Money: Bitcoin

Poloz, in the "what keeps him up at night" speech also said the Bitcoin frenzy worried him. Now of course, with the pandemic making teenage grocery store clerks afraid to touch dirty money, and the rest of us happy to use tap cards, digital money appears to be on the way.

Governments unhappy with companies like Facebook don't appear to want them advancing their digital currencies too far, and are suggesting that only governments should create currencies. Personally, I don't see how any corporation could control such a big part of a nation's economic sovereignty. And what if someone walks away with my life savings in digital currency. Is a mega tech company going to give my money back the way a government offers me deposit insurance? The digital giants sure can't give anyone their privacy back.

When only governments can take full accountability for a breakdown, they should have a heavy hand in the product. Beyond that, the Canadian dollar has provided us very worthy service, and, in recent years, enough so for more central banks abroad to stash Canadian dollars in their vaults as an asset on par with gold, U.S. dollars, euros, and yen as a very safe asset. Losing control of our currency as a dominant form of payment also means losing a lot of economic policy levers.

Central banks and other regulators around the world have made it clear that they see the dangers of unregulated digital money, and are also aware that popular demand may force it into existence. Their stand of suggesting that new forms of money must abide by the same rules as other players in the financial system seems like a minimum, if governments can enforce that.

One final argument for some caution with private digital money: most of us use credit and debt cards and other online forms of payment already, so the real value to consumers of a new form of digital money that isn't the Canadian dollar is questionable.

CHAPTER THIRTEEN

Decade of pain fades as rates climb back to 2008 levels

In January 2018, we ended one economic nightmare, having made enough progress for the Bank to make another rate increase to 1.25 percent. This was the highest borrowing cost since 2008, a sign of how long-lasting and damaging that global crisis was.

Growth was still limping along at 2.2 percent that year and 1.8 percent in 2019, for starters. Another risk the Bank put in the third sentence of its decision was the threat to NAFTA[4], without naming Donald Trump.

Another force suggesting rates wouldn't climb back up to normal was a somewhat new idea. With all these years of weak growth, the economy might now have more slack to grow without inflation becoming much of a problem. If true, this suggested low rates for even longer.

---

4   NAFTA: North American Free Trade Agreement

By now, many central banks outside Canada were having major difficul-ties pushing inflation back up to target. If the world wasn't going to see a wave of inflation, neither was Canada. Add on top of this the prior view that consumers would react very badly to even modest rate increases, and you could already guess that the terminal stop on this ride up wasn't going to be six percent.

"While the economic outlook is expected to warrant higher interest rates over time, some continued monetary policy accommodation will likely be needed to keep the economy operating close to potential and inflation on target. Governing Council will remain cautious in considering future policy adjustments, guided by incoming data in assessing the economy's sensitivity to interest rates, the evolution of economic capacity, and the dynamics of both wage growth and inflation."

By this time, there was a generation of Canadians who had never known anything but the lowest interest rates in modern history, and who had never had seen a jump in monthly payments. But the evidence for the idea that higher interest rates by themselves would trigger a consumer crunch has never really been tested.

Poloz vindication against surprised investors

In March 2018, three years after his surprise rate cut, Poloz got some recogni-tion as the publication "Central Banking" named the Bank of Canada the Bank of the Year. Poloz gave some insight on his thinking in response.

"We began talking about monetary policy as an exercise in risk manage-ment, as opposed to the precision engineering that many believe the practice of monetary policy to be. To be truly honest about the uncertainties we face, we stopped providing routine forward guidance, which observers and market participants had come to rely on. We took some grief for this decision. But I am certain that the best and most honest approach is to communicate openly about the Bank's reaction function, and the key risks we see. This leaves market participants to interpret the data and make their own forecasts about the future path of interest rates. It has taken time, but markets and observers are increasingly adapting to our approach."

It's a little funny now, looking at that last line about adapting. Markets certainly had to change how they looked at the Bank's "reaction function" after 2015. (The term "reaction function" is investor jargon for the idea that there is some kind of fixed strategy that will dictate how a central bank will respond to changes in the economy.)

Misgivings around private speeches

In his speech, Poloz also touted good communications and transparency. Here I must point out one of my personal bugaboos, the Bank's practice of giving private speeches. While we never really know the full extent of these, over time it's been revealed that at least several times a year, the Governor and the deputies speak at private gatherings, and sometimes to groups tied to financial markets. In an era of lower public trust in authorities, this seems risky.

I can see benefits of speaking privately to academics or some other groups, and the need to have private meetings with bank CEOs, for example, for candid exchange of views. But when it comes to speeches, the perception of speaking to investors who can trade off anything and pass themselves off as being in the know about what the Bank "really thinks" is corrosive to fairness. And while the Bank has repeatedly insisted that nothing market moving is ever said in private, it's a question of perception. Furthermore, to investors trading every day and reassessing new economic reports and other news, even a repetition of the central bank's thinking can be taken to mean that their view has withstood the latest report on jobs or inflation, which could have changed their thinking. One thing I can guarantee, if someone emailed me the text or a transcript of a private speech and I published it, even if it was almost a carbon copy of the last rate decision, it would probably move financial markets.

Around this time, the Bank made a big step forward. In the past, there was a delay between publishing a rate decision and economic forecasts, which could lead markets to re-interpret things in a way that was unwelcome. Then they changed to publishing them at the same time, and holding a press conference at four decisions (out of the eight) that came with that monetary policy report. But until this time, the other four decisions a year came only with the written statement. What if markets mis-interpreted those decisions? That could allow weeks, until the next scheduled speech, for things to fester. Now the Bank added "progress report" speeches the day after the shorter rate decisions, including a press conference. This came as other central banks were also seeking to become more transparent.

Closer to Home

With Poloz taking the Bank's reputation to a high-water mark, the key interest rate moved to 1.75 percent in October 2018. Canada now had one of the highest rates among big economies, and it was clear we were having better luck getting inflation up to around two percent.

After all the Trump drama, Canada had salvaged a trade deal with the U.S. and Mexico. Luckily, while Trump had threatened Canada, it seemed clear that Mexico was much more the target of his wrath. Canada's growth was still seen at a so-so two percent, enough to at least think prices wouldn't begin to sag.

"Given all of these factors, Governing Council agrees that the policy interest rate will need to rise to a neutral stance to achieve the inflation target. In determining the appropriate pace of rate increases, Governing Council will continue to take into account how the economy is adjusting to higher interest rates, given the elevated level of household debt. In addition, we will pay close attention to global trade policy developments and their implications for the inflation outlook."

Well, let's just say that, amid Trump's trade wars, Brexit, and continued weakness in the Eurozone and Japan, this wish for a neutral interest rate would not be realized.

Given the circumstances, while the economy didn't quite "come home," it had come to a decent place. Compared to other major economies, Canadians had much to be thankful for.

The job market as the economy rebalanced, and mythical labour shortages

In January 2019, Senior Deputy Carolyn Wilkins gave a speech about Canada's hot job market. Unemployment around this time was reliably around six percent or below, and that spring, it dropped to 5.4 percent, a modern day low. This was great news, but also puzzling because the economy wasn't that strong, and because wages were stagnant. This was another sign of the inability to generate inflation like major economies had done in the past. The implication for monetary policy was that high interest rates would not come back, and more emergency tools would become normalized.

Around this time, the creativity of industry groups and big companies complaining about workers also rose to new heights. We started publishing more data on "job vacancies," proving somehow that companies couldn't find workers with the "right skills," and implying this was somehow the government's or society's problem. I disagree.

If you're going to survey companies by asking if they can find all the workers they want with "day-one" skills, what do you expect them to say? In my view, these surveys overplay the idea of a labour "shortage."

If companies can't find workers at the prevailing wage, they can offer a higher wage to bring in workers. If they can't afford workers at just above the market wage, then the market is telling them the brutal truth—the products they make aren't competitive. Don't blame workers for your problems. Every industry group you will ever interview, when asked will say there is a skills shortage. Yet we know from research by the C.D. Howe Institute, hardly a communist organization, that Canada massively underinvests in equipment for employees relative to American competitors.

I've digressed a long way from what Ms. Wilkins said in her speech. Well, just a year later, unemployment would be a record high 13.7 percent, and much higher if you altered the tally to include more people on reduced hours or sitting out the pandemic. This reversal is perhaps another illustration of why governments must think carefully about spending money to help firms find skilled workers, since the needs of the market can change quickly.

Because it's 2019: Climate change comes to central banking

In March of 2019, the Bank of Canada joined a club of central banks studying climate change. For someone like me who was taught environmentalism in public school in the 1980s, this seemed obvious and overdue. If economists are scientific or dispassionate public policy makers, why did it take this long to get involved in the climate change file? Didn't the world identify climate change as a danger at least back to the Kyoto treaty? And therefore, shouldn't this have been incorporated into risk scenarios around that time?

Or more certainly, around the time scientists agreed we were a few degrees away from irreversible damage?

The arguments made in Canada and abroad—that central banks aren't really geared to set interest rates or broader policy on climate change—don't make sense to me. We've seen for a long time that insurance companies adjust premiums and coverage based on actual flood damage, not some hypothetical risk. Some major investors are also cutting back on investment in fossil fuel companies. There are real costs to the economy and to the public from climate change, and these can and should be measured.

Similarly, while the Bank of Canada joined a club of central banks looking at indigenous issues in 2021, the Minneapolis Fed already had a centre for indigenous development. No one in Canada needs to wait for a global consensus to emerge to tackle an economic problem, and the financial crisis of 2008 shows it's in our interest seek to be better.

If you see a central bank as a steward of the economy, and not as machine that resets interest rates every time you pull a lever, then surely it's clear the public is better off when a central bank outlines a global risk that individuals struggle to grasp.

The world is clearly going to change. Young people are already living in a world mostly without physical cash, and learning to live in a world where transportation is automated and not so reliant on fossil fuels.

CHAPTER FOURTEEN

Stumbling into 2020, then falling into it

The year 2019 closed with signs Canada's economy was sputtering, although not enough to cut rates. Donald Trump's shadow still loomed over global trade, hurting our exports and investment. There was some idea the Bank might cut if this continued. "Future interest rate decisions will be guided by the Bank's continuing assessment of the adverse impact of trade conflicts against the sources of resilience in the Canadian economy—notably consumer spending and housing activity. Fiscal policy developments will also figure into the Bank's updated outlook in January." Private economists were figuring the economy might stall out in the first quarter of 2020.

When 2020 came and we started hearing about a mystery virus, even if we thought it might be contained, the idea of China's economy going offline for a while suggested that a rate cut could be needed.

One illustration of how calm things were before Covid broke out was Poloz's Dec. 6 announcement that he wouldn't seek a second term. It's been a while since we had a two-term Governor, and Poloz had sprinkled his term with references to being a grandparent and hitting the golf course.

The year of 112 press releases

Here's one measure that gives a picture of 2020. The Bank of Canada posted 112 press releases, one every three days, on average. In 2019, for comparison, there were 64 press releases. The 2020 pace isn't desirable for an institution designed to move around mostly in the background and let Canadians sleep easy knowing inflation is stable.

In the short run, Covid-19 clearly tested the Bank of Canada to stabilize the economy and the government to save lives. In the long run, I wonder if people will become more cautious about traveling, and change their views of conspicuous spending after seeing mass unemployment, or become even more eager for bigger homes as a way of coping with a world of potential lockdowns. Or whether it could plunge people afterwards into greater risk-taking as they live for the now. Mostly, we all lost our sense of time as the division between work and home vanished, to almost a pre-industrial arrangement.

Social and economic policy have often changed after war or calamity in Canada. World War I brought us income tax, the Great Depression brought the Bank of Canada, World War II paved the way for the postwar consumerism and the expansion of federal powers. The 9/11 attacks brought in much more surveillance and security. I'm curious to see how Covid alters the economic landscape, particularly when it comes to work arrangements.

Early optimism on containing Covid

Well into February, I believed the virus would be contained, and Canada would do far better than most countries because we had experience with the SARS virus. Then suddenly things were closing down, and sometime in late February or March I left my office in the National Press Building, knowing I wouldn't be back for a long time. I came back once for a socially-distanced coffee with someone I had known forever and who I trusted, and for Bill Morneau's July fiscal "snapshot."

The year began with little sign that the 1.75 percent rate would be increased, and with some feeling it could be cut because of weakness, aside from the pandemic, that would emerge.

By late February, the news about Covid-19 was becoming extreme, and investors who remembered coordinated action around 2001 wondered if there would be a repeat to secure global confidence. Unlike 2001 when the world rallied to the U.S. cause, this time it appeared that America First policy and President Trump's wish to downplay the virus may have resulted in the U.S. waving away coordination.

We would quickly learn that the scale of the pandemic would require major action from every nation. Nations such as Iran and Italy suffered early, and there was early hope that perhaps other nations could do better and contain Covid-19.

On March 3, the Group of Seven major industrial democracies put out a somewhat odd statement saying that they "stand ready to cooperate" which was a backwards way of saying they were not directly cooperating.

From 1.75 percent to zero in no time

On March 4, at a regularly scheduled decision, the Bank of Canada cut the overnight interest rate by half a percentage point to 1.25 percent. Again, recall how rare it has been to move by half a point. In this case, you could argue that the economy was already weak and going half a point was justified by that slow momentum.

You could also cast your mind ahead not too far and see that, in any recession scenario, we were probably going to the record low 0.25 percent again.

It was clear that, given the timing of the pandemic, especially around March and onward, that GDP might hang on in the first quarter, but would surely decline in the second. In the early days, the Bank of Canada and the Fed were hanging on to the idea that the first wave could be wrapped up quickly, and the economy might get back on track again later in the year.

One problem for policy makers was that the 2020 economic downturn wasn't going to follow any playbook. Bad as 2008 and 2001 were, we had seen financial market crashes, terrorism, and war before. The big parallel everyone drew on was the Spanish Flu pandemic of 1918, but that was so long ago, it was hard to make any comparison. For one thing, Canada's economic statistics weren't the same as they are today, and of course, our medical system is more advanced. There were people who argued that the economy might react like it might after a big natural disaster, but really crises like Alberta's wildfires or the Quebec and Ontario ice storm were regional, and this was global.

It's quaint now to look at the March statement from the Bank of Canada about other forces going on in the economy, which the pandemic would later dominate. To be fair, no one knew what we were heading into. "It is becoming clear that the first quarter of 2020 will be weaker than the Bank had expected. The drop in Canada's terms of trade, if sustained, will weigh on income growth. Meanwhile, business investment does not appear to be recovering as was expected following positive trade policy developments. In addition, rail line blockades, strikes by Ontario teachers, and winter storms in some regions are dampening economic activity in the first quarter."

This kind of rate cut was again part of Poloz's risk management. Later, it would become what he would liken to a firefighter who would never be criticized for using too much water, an idea Tiff Macklem would also espouse when he took over. (Some investors would soon complain the Bank was using too much water, or more plainly, buying too many government bonds for the market to function.)

Poloz set down an early marker that the lender of last resort function might be brought out. (The lender of last resort is when the central bank essentially offers to buy almost any form of solid credit from banks to keep the financial system running.) "As the situation evolves, Governing Council stands ready to adjust monetary policy further if required to support economic growth and keep inflation on target. While markets continue to function well, the Bank will continue to ensure that the Canadian financial system has sufficient liquidity."

The frightening part of the market reaction when the pandemic hit full on were reports that government bond markets were freezing up, and it was unclear why. Remember that bond markets are often bigger than stock markets and government bonds are seen as the risk-free assets that are the benchmark for pricing just about everything else. Even the U.S. Treasury market, where investors put their money when they wanted unquestionable safety, seemed strained. Government of Canada bond markets had reports of similar strains. The demands to cash out also put strain on some of the world's biggest brokers to fill orders.

Unscheduled March 13 cut, and coordination with fiscal policy

On March 13, the Bank went even further with an unscheduled rate cut of half a percentage point. Again, extraordinary for the surprise and the scope of the reduction. Moreover, we were now in the territory of hosting joint press conferences to build public confidence. Poloz appeared with Finance Minister Bill Morneau and Superintendent of Financial Institutions, Jeremy Rudin. It's hard to believe that by December, all three of these top policy makers would be going or gone—Poloz as his term expired mid-year, Morneau dropped from cabinet amid political controversy in the summer, and Rudin in December, saying he would leave after serving out a term due to end in June 2021. Add to that CMHC's Evan Siddall moving out in 2021 and you have something of a decimation of economic policy makers.

The Bank noted not just the pandemic, but the plunge in crude oil prices, as Russia and Saudi Arabia fought over production controls, again. The Bank also gave guidance saying it "stands ready to adjust monetary policy further if required."

The lender of last resort powers then came online, with a facility to mop up short term business loans known as "bankers' acceptances."

The broader scope of the measures was impressive. OSFI chopped its capital requirements, allowing banks to lend hundreds of billions more, and the government created a series of new corporate credit programs. The government also quickly launched other big programs like a wage subsidy, the CERB[5] relief checks, and some measures for business rent relief.

While we did not have coordination at the international level, Canadian officials were all pulling together. The Bank later published this summary of its deliberations, and it's interesting to think about how much, under our framework with the Governor in charge, Poloz was taking in a lot of feedback from his deputies on this extraordinary day:

---

5   CERB: Canada Emergency Response Benefit

https://www.bankofcanada.ca/2020/03/summary-deliberations-governing
-council/

It's a long passage, but given the historic nature, worth reviewing:

> On the morning of March 13, the Governor and Senior Deputy Governor participated in a meeting with the Minister of Finance, the Deputy Minister of Finance, and the Superintendent of Financial Institutions. At that time, the Bank outlined its intention to introduce to the market a Bankers' Acceptance Purchase Facility to help relieve stresses in lending markets [...] At the same meeting, the Superintendent indicated that OSFI was prepared to announce a significant reduction in the domestic stability buffer to augment the lending capacity of Canadian banks; this followed similar moves in other major economies. Furthermore, the Minister of Finance stated his intention to introduce a significant fiscal stimulus in the following week. The Minister suggested that making a joint announcement of these moves by the Bank, OSFI and himself, later that same day, would be a powerful confidence-boosting statement for consumers, business, and financial markets. Interest rates were not discussed at that meeting.
>
> Later that day, the Governor and Senior Deputy Governor convened a meeting of Governing Council and briefed the other members about the impending announcements by other federal agencies. Although a revised staff projection was not yet available, it was evident to Governing Council that the disruptive impact of the coronavirus, along with the drop in oil prices, would in all likelihood justify some further easing of policy in the coming weeks [...]. In this context, the discussion moved to the question of the appropriate timing of any further interest rate adjustments: waiting until our next fixed announcement date in mid-April, when we would also have a new staff projection; waiting for another move in global interest rates, thereby

capitalizing on an international coordination effect, as we had done on March 4; or moving rates on Friday, thereby helping to create an even more powerful, domestically-coordinated policy package. After some discussion of the relative merits, Governing Council concluded that there could be considerable benefit to reducing interest rates immediately and significantly to complement the other measures supporting the functioning of credit markets. Accordingly, Governing Council decided on March 13 to reduce interest rates by 50 basis points.

The story for me had no nuance, in that sense making it easy to cover, but difficult in conveying how much was at stake. The exact timing of the announcements were surprises, but I knew that something big was coming from policy makers. My colleagues and I were already working at home, so we were around for breaking news more than we would be if we were commuting into work. The helpful thing some of us tried to do was to seek comparisons to the 1930s or to World War II. But the economic figures aren't directly comparable, and the pandemic was too new to know if those things are good comparisons, anyway.

Working from home, buyer of last resort

Like many others, I left my office in the National Press Building not knowing when I could come back. Little did I know I would be working at home almost every day for more than a year, or that I would be covering some of the biggest news of my career while also juggling children relegated to online classes with the same schedule of recess breaks and snack breaks as if they were in school, making me their lunch and hall monitor.

Only once did I shout my kids out of whatever room I needed to write up a breaking story. There were a few perks, like having a ready supply of the toys within easy reach of my laptop for comic relief. By this time, having gone through the bad experiences of 2001 and 2008, I was more able to be detached and have some perspective. I sprinted when I needed to sprint, but I also realized this was going to be a long-running story and it was best not to drain my batteries on any given day.

Through this time, the Bank of Canada started buying up lots of assets. I won't bore you with the details. The point is that with even the federal bond market, the bedrock of financial markets, cracking, the Bank of Canada saw the need to shore up corporate lending and provincial debt markets. It was never clear to me whether Newfoundland and Alberta, bearing the brunt of the pandemic *and* the oil price crash, were in edge-of-the-cliff kind of trouble in bond markets. I called both province's Finance Ministers and they declined to get back to me. The dollar value of the Bank's balance sheet moved to about 575 billion dollars in March 2021, from 125 billion dollars before the pandemic. While markets stabilized, in part because of the Bank's actions, the Bank later shifted the focus to say that its purchases would help hold down borrowing costs and therefore aid the economic comeback. Poloz at first also hesitated to call the program what it was, quantitative easing (QE).

In this case, the policy was needed because official interest rates were stuck as low as they could go. To hold down interest rates for companies and consumers, you just pump cash into the banking system and hope that works. The quantity of money itself becomes the policy. Bonds due in ten years can hardly be valued based on an overnight rate of interest in a crisis, but if the Bank of Canada buys up enough ten-year bonds, it can pull those yields down.

Through this era, I spoke to many former Bank advisers, mostly university professors, who questioned whether quantitative easing worked at all, or if the benefit compared to the effort and cost was small. Even its backers were reluctant to say this policy had a major impact. Then there is the question of whether we would ever get out of this emergency measure. After all, look at what happened in Europe and Japan, where asset purchases have gone on for quite a while, and even in the U.S., where the Fed never unwound its QE.

Given the public scrutiny that goes into how governments spend even a billion dollars on, for example, a train tunnel in Ottawa or a light rail system in Montreal, it makes me wonder if the scrutiny on using half a trillion dollars in financial markets is appropriately high.

With rates at zero, no other tools, and side effects

Again, the reason the Bank resorted to buying government bonds to hold down borrowing costs was that the regular benchmark interest rate was near zero and could go no lower. This is called the "zero lower bound" problem, and it's likely to remain a problem in future economic cycles. So if interest rates are unlikely to hold back up at five or six percent again to give a lot of breathing room, how much impact will monetary policy really have in the next downturn? In the world where quantitative easing becomes common, you now have proof that half a trillion dollars of asset purchases is how far you might have to go next time, too. But what if it requires a trillion? Is there any upper limit to how far we should go? Should a central bank be prepared to make larger purchases of corporate bonds next time as well?

Another issue about low and lower interest rates is that while it has pumped up the housing market, there's little real proof that it ever did much of anything to boost business investment or exports. While the economy may need a short term burst from ever more housing, in the long run, are we feeding a model of growth that's driven just by consumer debt?

These moves also raise political entrapment questions for the central bank. The federal government says it's relying on low interest rates to make its deficit spending affordable, and has put no plan in place to balance the books. So the central bank faces accusations of facilitating bad fiscal policy.

(Of course, there is a wider fiscal picture here. On a global scale, Canada has a top "triple-A" credit rating, and the scale of its deficits and debts are lower than most of its major peers, by most measures. Unlike the 1990s, when global bond markets looked at Canada with hesitation, today there's no question we can affordably finance large deficits. That was proven when Canada financed its record 327.7-billion-dollar deficit in fiscal 2020-21 amid the pandemic.)

The Bank has also argued it must be careful about raising interest rates because it may hurt heavily indebted consumers and slow the economy. What if that becomes the case for the federal government and its fiscal policy, too, constantly afraid to cut off vulnerable people?

The Covid recession has also opened the door to a modest plan to buy provincial debt, renewing questions about accountability and transparency. There could also be a perception that any provincial bond buying program was ramped up to save a couple of much weaker provinces. This would violate some sacred central bank orthodoxy about only fixing up illiquid borrowers, not insolvent ones. In other words, central banks can help borrowers who have a short-term financing problem but who are fundamentally sound, while avoiding aiding borrowers who have no future.

The Bank also made some waves when it cut rates to 0.25 percent again on March 27, calling it the effective lower bound. Yet a few years earlier, Poloz himself saw a research paper come out suggesting the rate could go to -0.5 percent with markets still functioning. Yes, negative 0.5 percent. Later, Governor Mackem also had some comments around negative rates being in the toolkit, but describing this as a distant possibility. Of course, in 2020, there seemed to be fewer and fewer distant possibilities.

Another tool that was brought out again was heavy forward guidance, though Carney's "conditional commitment" label was dropped. The Bank said it wanted to see the economy back at full potential and inflation sustainably at two percent before it could raise rates. Its own projections originally didn't see that happening until 2023, a forecast that would turn out to be terribly wrong.

On quantitative easing, the Bank said it would keep going until the recovery was "well underway." So here we move strongly in the direction of "judgment" over Poloz's "data dependency." A year later we still had no clear definition of what "well underway" meant.

By late in 2020, the Bank was able to scale back QE from at least five billion dollars a week to at least four billion dollars, and in spring of 2021, to three billion dollars. It later signaled that it could adjust again as it became more confident in the economy, thanks in large part to vaccine breakthroughs that solidified the economy's medium-term prospects. In the short term, GDP was shrinking early in 2021, based on the second wave of COVID-19.

So next time a central banker tells you they are "data dependent," remember that it all goes away in a pinch.

Of course, in a crisis, you do what you need to do. That's the evidence from the Bank, the finance department, and the bank regulator. They all moved fast and affirmed bold action.

On March 18, the Bank said most of its workers were now doing their jobs remotely.

It's worth repeating that all this happened between March 3 and March 18 of the year 2020. There was more news in these two weeks than you might normally get in two years!

To recap, the Bank made an unscheduled cut of half a percentage point to 0.25 percent, and, more importantly, they crossed the threshold into QE, with at least five billion dollars a week of federal debt, and with a signal there was more to come, if needed. "Governing Council stands ready to take further action as required."

The first draft of history, spoken by someone who's on mute

By this time, we were having a lot of press conferences by phone or video call instead of in person. For history's sake, I will remind future readers that remote press conferences have terrible limitations. Everyone forgets to turn their mute buttons on and off, everyone asks "can you hear me," and you have little idea dialing in how the moderator will take questions. At least once a month, you will be dropped from the question list for mysterious reasons. In the early days, I feared my cat or my child will make a terrible racket when I asked my question. (In my case, the name of my cat, Terry, is also the name of my company's CEO, so I doubly dreaded having to chastise my cat.)

The Bank of Canada's April 15 Monetary Policy Report declined to even give a standard economic forecast. For a central bank that boasts of having dozens of models and hundreds of economists, this was shocking, and more so considering private sector economists with far fewer resources were continuing to make forecasts.

The rate decision that day said, "Bank analysis of alternative scenarios suggests the level of real activity was down one to three percent in the first quarter of 2020, and will be fifteen to thirty percent lower in the second quarter than in fourth-quarter 2019. CPI inflation is expected to be close to zero percent in the second quarter of 2020."

The Bank was not willing to put the prospect of deflation on the table. It was hard for me to rule out at the time, but given the massive government income support, along with rising food prices, it wasn't really likely.

On the plus side, they didn't cut interest rates, holding them at 0.25 percent. Later, Macklem would suggest he could move rates in a micro cut of less than a quarter point, then thankfully, didn't. It's hard to see how such a small move would have done anything to boost public and business confidence.

Poloz retires, but an experienced Macklem is waiting to return

With Poloz's retirement coming up in June, the April meeting was one of his last scheduled meetings. On May 1st, Tiff Macklem was named the new Governor. Again, what's shocking about this is that, in normal times, this transition would have warranted months of media coverage. Given the circumstances (the pandemic), and besides, knowing Macklem had the experience to do the job, there wasn't much time to cover his takeover.

Carolyn Wilkins gave a speech three days later. Some reporters may have been disappointed that she kept the engagement and didn't complain about not getting the top job. However, it probably wasn't the year to bring open dissent to running the economy.

What is nice is that Canada has enough qualified people that we can consistently find a half dozen people who could be Governor tomorrow in a pinch and do the job well. While there might be people passed over, there has never been a sense that monetary policy has moved out of good hands.

Covid and touching cash

On May 28, the Bank put out a press release saying it was still as safe amid Covid to handle cash as anything else. It has become clear the people have spoken since then—most stores only offer up tap machines for credit and debit cards, and a few stores I've been into specifically ask you not to pay in cash if possible. There has been talk about the pandemic accelerating trends around both remote work and the shift away from cash, and I suspect that younger people will have no problem without cash. Will future generations understand this sentence at all? "My grandmother mailed me a birthday card with a twenty-dollar bill in it; I should telephone her to say thank you." I don't know how digital money is coming along, but it seems like it must be on the way. The Bank's own surveys show eighty percent of people have no plans to give up cash, but that also suggests that twenty percent are thinking about it. That would have been impossible a generation ago.

Macklem tells Fed about populism amid Trump, Wilkins leaves

In July 2020, the bank held rates and QE again, and showed some optimism that the economy was opening again. Of course, no one could predict that the second wave would be worse than the first.

Also in July, Macklem spoke at the Federal Reserve's Jackson Hole conference to sell the need for central bank transparency in an age of populist anger, and it will be interesting to see where all that goes, both in the U.S. and in Canada. Central banks seem vulnerable to these kinds of attacks against experts, especially with the surge of inflation we've seen following the end of Covid lockdowns.

In September, Carolyn Wilkins announced she would not seek a second term when hers ran out on May 1. On Nov. 5, she said she was leaving on Dec. 9, carrying through the last rate decision of the year. For "Bank watchers," this was hard to ignore. More obviously, the Governing Council had lost its only woman, and had no visible minorities. Hard not to notice against a female Finance Minister and a feminist Prime Minister. Wilkins also had a big hand in overseeing the financial plumbing before and after the 2008 crisis, knowledge that's hard to replace.

The October decision showed decisively that quantitative easing was the new dominant monetary policy. The Bank said it was calibrating the program to four billion dollars a week from five billion. More of the focus would be on longer term assets, allowing the bank to argue that "quantitative" easing was in fact becoming more "qualitative," and by this shift it would better target where most lending to firms and households really took place.

This, to me, did two things. It showed that bond purchases were no longer essential to keep the banking system running smoothly. Instead, the Bank was now pumping money into the economy to keep it afloat. The second thing it did was address a potential political concern about 2008-style bank bailouts. The intention of the policy now was to lower borrowing costs for businesses and households. Most mortgages have five-year terms and many business loans are also around this length of time, so seeking to keep borrowing costs low for five-year loans wasn't just good for banks, it was good for entrepreneurs and families. This was an argument overlooked in subsequent debates about the merits or the dangers of what some politicians called "printing money" and creating reckless inflation.

We wrap 2020 with rates at 0.25 percent, four billion dollars a week of asset purchases, and this extraordinary guidance.

> Canada's economic recovery will continue to require extraordinary monetary policy support. The Governing Council will hold the policy interest rate at the effective lower bound until economic slack is absorbed so that the two percent inflation target is sustainably achieved. In our October projection, this does not happen until into 2023. To reinforce this commitment and keep interest rates low across the yield curve, the Bank will continue its QE program until the recovery is well underway and will adjust it as required to help bring inflation back to target on a sustainable basis. We remain committed to providing the monetary policy stimulus needed to support the recovery and achieve the inflation objective.

This is another long bridge to cross without raising interest rates. A few economists early in 2021 had already explicitly forecast a rate increase late in 2022, already setting up another round of wondering if interest-rate commitments work, and if they are worth keeping to the end. Later, Macklem shifted forward the conditional commitment to the "middle quarters" of 2022 and then hiked rates in March 2022.

Investors didn't question this sequence because inflation had surged so much as the economy re-opened after Covid, and inflation surged to six percent. Perhaps the lesson for markets is that as long as they think they are anticipating what's happening, they don't care so much about the Bank's commitments. But for me, we have two clear cases now where the Bank's pledges to hold rates in a downturn have ended early. So if this tool is used again, will it be as effective? What I have observed so far is that markets have leaned toward the forgiving side, and quickly moved on from this question.

The era closes with a watered-down inflation mandate

To close out this difficult year, the Bank made a fundamental change to its mandate in December 2021, heavily influenced by the pandemic.

Agreements with the government on inflation date back to 1991, when there were fears the GST would add to woes from Canada's weak economy to drive inflation way up. The targets worked so well they were quickly adopted, and held at two percent. Following that, there were few major changes during renegotiations with the government done every five years. These talks are a valuable way to make sure the Bank of Canada remains accountable to Parliament on the big issues, without politics cramping how Governors implement their mandate.

This time was a little different than the usual rubber stamp of a single inflation target. Governor Tiff Macklem and Finance Minister Chrystia Freeland tweaked the language to say that the Bank will now seek full employment so long as it respects its inflation goal. While this isn't a "dual mandate" for stable prices and full employment like the U.S. Federal Reserve has, it certainly expands the mandate and creates some temptation to cheat on inflation.

The potential dangers of this are perhaps being seen now with the Bank of Canada turning into the most aggressive central bank among G7 nations in 2022, with three percentage points of rate hikes between March and September, admitting inflation will average six percent in the first half of the year and not return to two percent until 2024. Unemployment also fell to the lowest since the 1970s; the economic rebound from Covid was faster than expected. Suffice it to say that making such a big shift to tightening monetary policy less than a year after relaxing the inflation mandate is not the best look.

In other words, just as the Bank of Canada and the government set the table to have potentially looser policy to chase full employment, inflation surged with a vengeance. Only time will tell if an adjustment will be needed after this economic cycle to restore a pure inflation mandate.

On the facts of the inflation surge and whether the Bank of Canada waited too long to address it, we have to remember the situation at the time. The pandemic was still quite unknowable in terms of whether the next wave would again fill up hospitals and force provinces to shut down most businesses and schools. The Bank of Canada simply could not have known, even in January 2022 when it held rates instead of hiking, that the economy would be so resilient as omicron variant of Covid swept over us, or what Russia would do to Ukraine.

So anyone with the idea that the Bank was "behind the curve" around the end of 2021 and into early 2022 must ask themselves if they would have been willing to tell Canadians, who were facing a truck protest that threatened to overthrow the government, a bleak winter, and the omicron wave, that this was a really strong economy in need of major tightening. That said, it was clear from the Bank's own quarterly Business Outlook Survey that, around this time, inflation expectations were getting quite hot. But given the potential for the economy to fall into another big lockdown, an even bigger mistake might have been to put the brakes on the economy.

CHAPTER FIFTEEN

Future issues for the Bank

Global populism and mistrust of experts

Just as the media, as an institution, has been threatened and weakened by social media and a wave of global political populism, the Bank of Canada has also been under more pressure. Some of this is legitimate scrutiny, while some of it could be destabilizing.

Opposition Members of Parliament have recently been asking tougher questions about policies such as quantitative easing, which I have said elsewhere in this book is largely a plausible idea. Some of the questions have been a bit off-base factually, but that could just be the difficulty of the material. Parliament is an important way of bridging the divide between the experts at the central bank and the public's questions. There is also an element of hostility in some recent cases, which in the past was quite rare for Bank of Canada Governors to encounter. I'm not sure the Bank of Canada is well equipped for this kind of political debate.

The Bank has done some things to get its message out to the public that are very good. It's using social media more, and its speeches now come with plain language summaries. But to keep public trust, more work may be needed. The low level of public awareness of monetary policy coupled with angrier political populism could lead to sudden and unwelcome change.

From a more demanding public, it's possible for some healthy change. There is a view that monetary policy is mostly about making technical adjustments to an economic machine, and questions about orthodoxy and perceptions of a lack of transparency can be brushed off. But just as some people want corporations to be more than "sharks" just eating up as much profit as they can, the Bank of Canada could be more a steward of a strong economy. David Dodge once quipped that no one ever compliments the Bank for organizing a really good bond auction. Doing a sound technical job isn't enough for people to think you are good at your job. The Bank has a lot of knowledge about the wider economy that it could do a better job of sharing with the public.

Pierre Poilievre's call to fire the Governor

I must address the controversy in 2022 when Conservative Party leadership candidate Pierre Poilievre said he would fire Governor Tiff Macklem for missing the surge in inflation and for being pushed into underwriting government deficits. (Most of this book was written before he made those comments.)

Recall what the Bank of Canada Act says about the terms of the Governor's employment. The Governor serves subject to "good behaviour" for seven years, and the Finance Minister must consult cabinet if there is a major disagreement, and then send a formal directive to Parliament. While the letter of the law says a Governor must comply with a directive from the government, in practice the Governor would almost certainly quit.

Let's look in more detail about the arguments made in favour of removing the Governor.

Experts say no one could have predicted the Covid pandemic or the Russian attack on Ukraine, and these two things account for most of the inflation seen in Canada and around the world. That is mostly true.

Some critics, even many middle-of-the-road economists, say the Bank should have acted faster. They quickly forgot how glum things were, even early in 2022 when hospitals overflowed with people suffering from the omicron variant of Covid. Raising interest rates amid this misery and uncertainty would have been heartless.

There is also a big question of hypocrisy among parliamentarians who suggest that the Bank of Canada's monetary stimulus was solely to blame for any run-up in prices.

The minority Parliament that could have dictated pandemic spending policies to Justin Trudeau instead handed the Liberal government nearly unlimited spending powers, and seemed to ask few questions about a substantial pullback in record deficit spending. Conservatives under Erin O'Toole also campaigned on a running decade of budget deficits. The NDP pushed for the expansion of public services and more generous relief payouts. So the idea that the Bank of Canada was riding in solo, delivering massive stimulus, and that Parliament can claim innocence, is a big fish to swallow whole.

Again, the merits of stimulus to keep infected people from going to work and spreading a disease so deadly the army ended up going into some seniors' residences is a debate for all Canadians. So is the debate over how many people were enticed to draw on CERB payments they didn't desperately need, or beyond the point where they could have safely gone back to work.

When we look outside Canada, there is some evidence we were not a singular over-spender. Canada's fiscal response was, in the end, seemingly smaller than what the U.S. brought in with its trillion-dollar relief packages. And in the beginning of Covid, some European countries offered a much larger wage subsidy to keep people on the payroll of companies, and arguably this was needed to avoid people going straight to traditional relief payouts.

I also find it a reach to say the Bank of Canada's bond purchases were designed primarily to help the government borrow cheaply. The clear aim of the program was firstly to ensure the banking system didn't freeze up, and then to lower borrowing costs for all Canadian households, and to help companies to create jobs. Given that government bonds are the foundation of financial markets, you simply cannot help Canadians without acting to lower federal government bond yields. Well, there are a few ways, but they are even more perilous: who wanted to see the Bank's program of buying corporate bonds expanded even further than it was? Or have the government pick even more winners and losers?

There is no question that using large-scale government bond purchases (Quantitative Easing), which was used by other major central banks in the 2008 crash (but not Canada's), was a new and untested tool that deserves close political scrutiny. The Bank's balance sheet swelled from 125 billion to 575 billion dollars in short order. The justifications also changed from stabilizing markets, which at the peak of the crisis was quite true—even the massive U.S. Treasury market was freezing up. After that, it was used as more traditional economic stimulus, which according to the Bank's own research, only lowered borrowing costs a little bit. It's more than fair to ask why hundreds of billions of dollars of public resources should be used for so little return, and I have yet to hear an answer that's equal to that outlay.

Poilievre also says the Bank of Canada's purchases of government bonds and "printing money" made it easier to finance record budget deficits. He appears to suggest Justin Trudeau's fiscal recklessness amounted to pressure on the central bank to follow his lead.

There isn't a lot of evidence that the quantitative easing program made much difference to the federal government's borrowing costs. Government bond yields had already been at or near record lows for quite a while before the pandemic, so the Bank's actions were much less substantial than meets the eye. Simply put, governments could already borrow for very little, with or without the Bank's bond purchases. The federal government's credit ratings for the most part remained at the highest level before and after the pandemic. My own observation was that before Covid, some government bond yields were regularly below two percent, so there was a long window to run even more aggressive deficits at low cost.

While the effect of the QE policy was small for government borrowing costs, and by extension for the rest of us, at the time, small business groups said they needed any help they could get. Every week, there were some firms deciding to go bankrupt, while others were borrowing heavily, hoping they could survive the shutdowns. We can question the hundreds of billions of dollars of public resources used under quantitative easing for such a small return in lowering yields, but I'm not sure this rises to a firing offense. Central banks are there to be a "lender of last resort," and the numbers of dollars at stake are always going to be large. To restrict the central bank's ability to tackle a crisis is a shift back to the laissez-faire policies of the 1930s Great Depression, which, by the way, convinced past governments to create the Bank of Canada. Again today, voters and Parliament must decide what was justified in an economic crisis.

On the other hand, if the bond purchases only lowered market interest rates by so little, can we really buy the critics' argument that the Bank of Canada's actions led to a major rise of inflation?

Another factor to consider when looking at whether the Bank of Canada's extraordinary actions underwrote Trudeau's deficits: the bonds purchased were already trading in the market; they were not new bonds sold to cover new expenses. New bonds were sold directly to private investors, who had no obligation to buy at any price. Again, bond yields through most of the pandemic stayed near record lows, and today they are still not high, by historical standards. If Wall Street believed Canada was going bankrupt, they would have signaled that loud and clear. But with U.S. fiscal policy so much more aggressive, with trillion-dollar rescue packages, Canada didn't seem so bad. Historically as well, this stance was less active than, for example, the Bank's role in managing government bonds around World War II.

Poilievre also wants to fire Governor Tiff Macklem for the bond purchases. The purchases were started and most were implemented by Governor Stephen Poloz, who was appointed by Stephen Harper's government. Macklem inherited this program in the middle of a pandemic and stayed the course. It would have been destabilizing to repudiate the purchases in the middle of Covid. In fact, Macklem soon turned to scaling back the purchases as the economy improved, then he halted net new purchases, and now is unwinding quantitative easing as maturing bonds come due. Painting Macklem as someone who was eager to expand this program just doesn't fit the facts.

Again, we can argue that the pace of Macklem's transition away from bond purchases is too slow, and I would suggest there's nothing wrong with actively selling off these bonds as fast as we bought them, but it's harder to argue that Macklem is fundamentally out of bounds.

Another way of looking at whether the bond purchases were justified is the actions taken by other global central banks. Canada avoided using QE in the 2008 downturn, which was triggered by bad mortgage loans and bank collapses in the U.S., the U.K., and parts of Europe. During Covid, Canada joined in the use of quantitative easing along with the vast majority of our peers. This was in part because global interest rates had gone through a long-term decline, so traditional monetary policies of cutting borrowing costs had been exhausted. Canada, like other central banks early in the pandemic, simply ran out of room to stimulate the economy by lowering interest rates; it's fair to say it would have been rightly criticized for not using other tools. The evidence for whether Canada did more or less with QE than others is somewhat mixed, but it's fair to say that, overall, Canada is not an outlier in how much stimulus was brought in under QE. The Bank of Canada has also tightened somewhat more quickly than its peers.

As for missing the inflation jump, this was true early in the economic rebound from Covid. Most economists in the public and private sectors, in Canada and abroad, missed it, too. Much of the rise in prices comes from global commodities like energy and food, not domestic policy actions. The causes of inflation were sudden, unpredictable, and novel. The Covid pandemic, supply bottlenecks across global supply chains, and the war in Ukraine all raised prices.

The way the government has worked to define the Bank of Canada's role in guarding against rapid inflation gives some idea about whether it has been a fundamental failure. The government gives the Bank of Canada a written mandate on how to tackle inflation, which is renewed every five years. The agreements put in some insulation against the Bank being a scapegoat for sudden or short-term price swings.

The inflation-targeting agreements signed with Conservative and Liberal Finance Ministers have run for three decades now. The simple fact that the overall system has stood up for decades, through several opportunities for bigger changes, and through governments of different stripes, should be a testament that the system works.

Most of this time, the government and Bank of Canada have stuck with targeting the year-over-year change in the consumer price index at two percent. The CPI is the most basic measure of overall inflation, and is published independently by Statistics Canada, so the public can be assured there will be no fudging the goalposts. Under these agreements, the Bank is expected to bring things back to target within two years, not six months as some critics appear to expect today. There is a very good reason why the Bank of Canada needs that timeframe to do its job.

While changing interest rates can have some immediate effect on the economy by moving the Canadian dollar and short-term lending rates, the full impact on the real economy can take over a year and likely two years to be felt. For example, employers usually adjust wages once a year, suppliers often need time to adjust their prices, and that takes even more time to be seen at the retail level. On that basis, monetary policy can't be faulted for failing to account for a shift in the economy until it has the chance to do something about it.

We can argue about the speed and timing of the Bank's reaction, but based on the mandate agreed upon with Parliament, there has been no fundamental breach of trust. Some would argue the failure of execution so far is bad enough, but this must be weighed against whether it was reasonable to delay action amid the pandemic and the early days of the Russian invasion of Ukraine. In short, unless inflation persistently holds above two percent and the Bank has no real plan to bring it back to normal, it has wide latitude to argue it's following its remit.

Parliament and the Bank of Canada had the choice all the way back to the origin of inflation targets in the 1990s to set a tougher standard that would force the Bank to set monetary policy to correct past misses on inflation. This was always judged to be too rigid, forcing the Bank to potentially trigger a recession every time there was a short-term jump in prices.

In other words, past governments have not set a standard that requires the Bank of Canada to carry a significant burden for any past errors. As long as the Bank seeks to return inflation to two percent, there is no clear legal mechanism for the government to interfere in the central bank's work.

Since inflation has surged in 2022, the Bank has taken important corrective action. Its own forecasts in mid-2022 show that policy makers realize inflation will likely not return to target within two years, and they have started to raise interest rates accordingly. The July 2022 interest-rate increase of 100 basis points is unheard of under the current policy framework, showing how seriously policy makers take the inflation risks now.

The Bank of Canada did show some weakness when it veered towards calling inflation transitory, a view that relied too much on traditional economic models that they should have known might have given a false reading in response to such a large economic shock. This was also a mistake made in the U.S. and elsewhere around the world.

Underlying Poilievre's case is the idea that "gatekeepers" can and should be sacked to improve the economy, and in a way, saying that monetary policy should not be independent of the government of the day. Most nations around the world have sought to put monetary policy in outside hands, the simple reason being that any government heading to an election would prefer a red-hot economy and low interest rates, and worry about any burst of inflation after they win power again.

The Bank of Canada Act enshrined some real protections against this kind of problem. Governors serve seven-year terms that outlast any one elected government. The Governors are nominated by an outside board of directors by cabinet, through the Finance Minister. The Bank's budget is also fairly autonomous, more evidence that Parliaments of the past saw interference as something not to be taken lightly. In practice, the Finance Minister and Governor talk to each other regularly to avoid any kind of fundamental misunderstanding.

As already noted, the way to dismiss a Governor is by making a public declaration in Parliament, so Canadians will be able to see the reasoning and judge the new direction of policy. That tool has never been used in its current form.

Do Canadians want to set a new precedent here, that missing the inflation goal after a rebound from a massive recession after using agreed-upon tools can result in the Governor being dismissed? If so, the next agreement on inflation targets may need to codify such an approach, but it's hard to imagine a credible regime that could spell that out.

As this book argues, the scope of monetary policy is quite different in a crisis than in normal times. If the Bank abused QE in a more regular economic cycle, there were large deficits, and the economy overheated, that would be more like a breach of trust. In a crisis, you must take strong action and there will be over-calibration.

While Parliament must retain and be prepared to exercise full authority over monetary policy, it's also wise to have a high bar for ordering a change of direction. I also suspect the next government would have a hard time taking its own medicine and ordering the Bank of Canada to slow down the economy and the job market at any cost until inflation reached two percent, especially in any future minority Parliament.

Canada isn't alone in having a major politician calling for the firing of the central bank chief. In the U.S., Donald Trump also threatened to fire Jerome Powell. This created some uncertainty in financial markets and the same could be true in Canada if we moved down that path. The U.S. Congress later confirmed Powell for a second term in a landslide vote, by the standards of these partisan times.

Our country, in the past, also went through some damaging angst around tensions between John Diefenbaker's government and former Governor James Coyne. Out of that painful time emerged law and tradition that makes two things clear: the Bank of Canada Governor is accountable to Parliament through the Finance Minister and cabinet, who can publish a directive stating the disagreement. Governors are traditionally understood to know they would almost certainly have to resign in such a case, though this has not been put to the test.

This is an important arrangement. It ensures that in a democratic society, elected lawmakers can take ultimate responsibility for the work of a public institution like the central bank. It also ensures that Governors can carry out their job over the agreed-upon seven-year term and subject to the written mandate to target two percent inflation, without much interference. Both sides know they will pay a heavy price if a Governor is removed, and gives strong incentives to avoid this outcome.

Governments should remember that removing a Governor is a very serious matter to investors and the public. It's hard to make a case that Tiff Macklem has performed worse than his international peers, or that Canada's inflation problem is his alone to solve.

Big and sudden changes may also create bad perceptions outside Canada. Nations that recently dismissed central bank chiefs include: Guinea, Iran, Myanmar, Syria, Turkey, Yemen. Joining this group won't speak to our economic freedom or stability.

A last note: one role of a journalist is to be an observer of powerful people and help relay who they are. Before Macklem was Governor, he was my dinner date for the Press Gallery Dinner in Ottawa, and I have seen him around in other situations. If the accusation is that he's a member of the elite or a gatekeeper, I can say through first hand observation that I've never seen him deride Canadians, put his own perks ahead of the work at hand, or be a political partisan.

Singh's call to change the Bank's mandate

The Bank of Canada then came under attack from the political left.

On Oct. 19, 2022, New Democratic Party Leader Jagmeet Singh included these attacks on the Bank of Canada during Question Period in an exchange with Prime Minister Justin Trudeau.

> Given the fact that the increased interest rates of the Bank of Canada will not address the root causes of inflation, they are certainly going to create a self-induced recession, which will result in massive job losses. Does the Prime Minister agree with the Bank of Canada's approach?

And following up:

> Mr. Speaker, New Democrats have a rich tradition of calling out institutions that end up exploiting or hurting people. It is clear that the Government of Canada sets the mandate. Now, this very same Bank of Canada's Governor has stated to employers that they are discouraged from increasing wages to keep up with inflation, which is ludicrous because there is absolutely no evidence that high wages have in any way contributed to inflation. In fact, wages have not kept up with inflation historically. Does the Prime Minister agree with the Bank of Canada's discouraging employers from increasing wages to keep up with inflation?

The NDP has a supply-and-confidence agreement to prop up Trudeau's minority government, so this carries some more immediate political tension. (The Bloc Quebecois, as of November 2022, had not made any similar attack.) Trudeau and Finance Minister Chrystia Freeland defended the Bank's independence and its work, as they are more or less obliged to do in Parliament. (Remember that the power of a directive to change course is delivered through

Parliament, so failing to support the Bank is hardly an option.) Singh later told reporters he doesn't want the Governor fired, but the Bank's mandate should be changed to put more emphasis on full employment.

Recall that less than a year ago, the government and Bank published a revised inflation targeting agreement giving the Bank scope to seek maximum employment, but only when the inflation target is well in hand. The December 2021 statement said this: "Given that there is uncertainty about the maximum level of employment that is consistent with price stability, the Bank will continue to use the flexibility of the 1 to 3 percent control range to actively seek the maximum sustainable level of employment when conditions warrant."

Taking Singh's arguments in order, the idea that interest rates won't tackle the root cause of inflation has some only very limited merit. He doesn't identify what the root cause of inflation is, but in other comments has spoken of "greed-flation" sparked by companies taking advantage of the pandemic.

While most economists don't identify price gouging as the prime driver of inflation, there has been a global discussion about how inflation is being caused both by supply and demand, and how that affects a central bank's effectiveness with higher interest rates. On the supply side, the disruptions from Covid and the Ukraine war to production and delivery of goods and services is more difficult to address with interest rates. Monetary policy can't re-open factories in China or unload cargo in Montreal. On the demand side, the rush to return to travel, restaurants and other activities after lockdowns ended is seen as pushing up prices for some goods, and here, higher interest rates do perform a more traditional role in making sure the economy doesn't remain over-stretched.

You can argue about whether it's supply or demand (or gouging) causing inflation, or how effective rate hikes will be, given the mix of these forces. What's harder to argue with is the idea that central banks still have the luxury of choosing a loose policy. Inflation is no longer the "transitory" force the experts thought it was early in the economic rebound from Covid. Price gains are now broad and persistent, and letting inflation run at a fast pace creates the danger of a dreaded "wage-price spiral" or another sequence where people keep pushing up prices simply because they expect prices to keep rising. Canadians watching bidding wars on houses in Vancouver and Toronto, and more recently even in cottage country, know what this pattern looks like. Central banks also learned a hard lesson in the 1970s about how difficult it can be to push inflation back down to a reasonable level once expectations of price increases become entrenched; this is exactly what Governor Macklem has been arguing. Remember, as well, that the Bank's job is to pull inflation back down to two percent from about eight percent, and its forecast is that it will take until the end of 2024 for that to happen. This doesn't suggest an easy trade-off by which policy makers can tilt the scales towards job creation.

Singh also says the Bank will create self-induced recession with a lot of job losses; he also at other times has said this kind of a recession would be needless.

There is a good deal of thinking around the idea that a recession in Canada would not be driven exclusively by tighter monetary policy. In the second half of 2022, the IMF and many private economists began to forecast the global economy tipping towards a recession. Many think that Canada, by virtue of its being a trade-dependent economy, would face a hit to growth from the global backdrop, and higher interest rates hitting housing and consumer spending would also play a key part. The government agreed with the Bank that fiscal policy should not add to inflation pressures, against Singh's wish for more government support.

As for massive job losses, as of October 2022, the unemployment rate was close to the record low 4.9 percent set earlier in the year. Canada has also more than recovered all the jobs lost during the pandemic. While Singh's suggestion is more about where the job market is heading, there's little question that the starting point is a job market that's strong and incredibly resilient through a global pandemic. That tends not to suggest the need for an extra nudge from monetary policy.

The word "recession" is also misleading in this context, given that the economy is still not in a traditional economic cycle of expansion and recession, but rather being dominated by shocks from the pandemic lockdowns and the Ukraine war. These are adjustments in the real economy caused by changed rules of work, physical shortages of commodities destroyed in war, and production being re-aligned after a pandemic.

You can't really have a recession when unemployment might simply be moving from a record low to something more normal, and home prices move from highly overvalued to less so. So if this isn't a regular recession, it's not quite fair to demand the Bank of Canada change its mandate.

Singh is correct to observe that the Bank's current mandate doesn't require it to account for a recession directly; rather, its mandate is to remain focused on inflation. He is also more on topic in seeking a mandate change. However, at this point, it would feel more like a directive to open up the mandate in the middle of a crisis to satisfy one opposition party. It's unclear how financial markets would react, but it's hard to see a very positive response in the short term, and easy to see a loss of investor confidence in the longer term.

On the idea of making the Bank of Canada like the Fed, with a "dual mandate" for inflation control and maximum employment, some economists have already questioned this. The main problem is that the Bank has one blunt tool to control the economy, it's the trend-setting interest rate. It's hard to chase two goals with one tool, and there is real danger that, by chasing both, you accomplish neither.

The Bank's interest rate increases are sharp, but they are aimed to match a sharp rise in inflation that is dominating people's everyday lives. The Bank has an obligation to put this behind us.

One last note about calls from lawmakers to improve monetary policy. The effectiveness of monetary policy rests in large part on the efficiency of the wider economy. An economy with a responsive job market, an education system creating skilled workers, competitive exporters, and sound financial markets, will transmit signals from monetary policy much more effectively. Much of that rests on what the federal and provincial governments do.

Looking at the arguments from the political left and right, it's clear that high inflation is creating a lot of misery for Canadians. This comes after a global pandemic that was traumatic for many. Following two years without nice vacations or date nights, seeing the cost of most goods rising faster than most of us can remember or easily afford is upsetting. In a democratic society, the Bank must be accountable, and it is responsible for communicating plainly and fairly with Canadians. People can argue whether it's fair to blame the Bank of Canada chief and dismiss him. What is required is more of a case showing that the Bank's actions fell outside its parliamentary mandate, and how bringing in another Governor or a new mandate would lead to a better outcome. Ministers in Ottawa rarely lose their jobs merely because something bad happened on their watch, let alone for policies that happened under previous management. The ministerial standard for dismissal seems to be a deeper mismanagement or insensitivity. I have not seen evidence that the Bank of Canada has been callous with Canadians, or blind to the dangers of high inflation. Finally, countries that dismiss central bank Governors often face some backlash in global financial markets, and Canada's reputation as a stable place for business may suffer from anything other than an airtight shift in the direction of monetary policy.

In the end, it's up to all Canadians to decide what they want from their central bank in the future. That debate should look for solutions that will last through a future crisis, not one that seems to carry us through the current one.

Climate change

Central banks have been too slow to account for climate change damage to the economy. The Bank itself overlooks the Ottawa River, flooded twice in recent years. Insurance companies are also able to calculate costs through higher claims and higher premiums. We may also see the auto industry go electric before central banks specifically map out how climate change will upend the economy. With experts saying we are only a few degrees of warming away from a major breakdown, the Bank has only started to figure out ways to embed these risks and costs into its economic framework.

Rational economists don't wait for the government to act to lay out the facts of climate change. The idea of "externalities," or costs that exist in the world but escape the realm of markets and fester in the background, is standard fare in undergraduate economics textbooks. Scientific consensus said, well before 2020, that we were just a few degrees from incredible damage. The Bank could be much further along in doing this work, which has implications for the economy's performance and financial market stability.

Housing strains

The housing boom, and the run-up of prices in Toronto and Vancouver, especially, is going to be with us for a long time. Someone who took out a big mortgage in 2010 or 2015 when things started getting very hot, likely with a twenty-year amortization, will be paying it off into 2030 and beyond. There are potential distortions to disposable income, and "house poor" people long into the future; this disrupts consumer spending. Very expensive housing in major cities is also now a social problem of affordability, and governments remain keen to help first-time homebuyers and other select groups; this will be at odds with financial regulators trying to keep a lid on things. The Bank of Canada will also continue to struggle with the trade-off of boosting growth with low rates and the lopsided consumer-heavy growth that results.

On the other side of the coin, experts have been warning of the dangers of a hot housing market all the way back in back to 2009 after the U.S. market collapsed, and in Canada we are still talking about it today without having seen a crash. At this point, any collapse that happens is not exactly a bubble like the one we imagine in the stock market. It could truly be a more secular, long term trend.

That also means the dangers aren't going away. It might be helpful to the Bank of Canada and the public at large if responsibility for taming any housing market excess was taken on more explicitly by the government. If Canadians decided they don't want to eat soup for a year to save a bigger down payment on a house; they want thirty-year mortgages; they want a house that costs a million dollars; that's a fundamental change that can't be smoothed out with a couple of rate hikes. Maybe the government could put a higher floor on mortgage rates, or require twenty-five percent down payments.

That said, the Bank can't escape the links between a long period of rock-bottom interest rates and the growth in housing. The Bank argues that it's the "last line of defense" on housing pressures. With home prices rising so much, even the last line of defense should be getting a little nervous. The bias we seem to have—public policy seeking to boost employment and investment even if it balloons consumer debt—is becoming less and less comfortable.

If the Bank can take credit for the good economic times, they must also look hard at today's housing crisis, especially in their role as an economic steward.

There are no easy answers to the obvious thing: affordability has slipped away in Vancouver and Toronto, and million-dollar houses require million-dollar mortgages.

The inflation mandate

In the next renewal of the inflation mandate, a future government will decide whether it was unwise to add full employment language to the two percent inflation goal, or if there needs to be a more explicit commitment on climate change or digital currency. I certainly don't think it should take on a full employment mandate like the U.S. Fed has.

If you recall high school algebra, the formula that links inflation and interest rates is straightforward. You raise interest rates, companies and people borrow less and spend less, demand for goods wanes, and inflation slows. In other words, interest rates can do that job over time.

But think about the equation you might write to define what can influence unemployment across an economy; it's a much longer equation.

Job creation depends on productivity of labour, business investment, economic growth, and interest rates, but also the global economy, the currency, the population's education. With the focus in the last year around improving employment by gender and race, there seems to be some implicit pressure to go beyond what monetary policy can safely accomplish.

There is a danger that the goals around inflation and the job market come into direct conflict, in the case where inflation is too high, yet the job market is still weak, for example. Interest rates can't be in two places at the same time, so one of the goals would be undermined. Investors would figure this out in minutes and react accordingly, and the Bank would lose credibility and its ability to fight either battle and win.

Rather than making this a central bank responsibility, companies and governments have a role to play. The levers for making people employable are education and skills. We know Canadian firms invest much less in training than U.S firms do. I await the world where "lifelong learning" is really a thing. While some people manage to grab an executive MBA mid-career and leap forward, how many of us can do that? More to the point, the iconic laid off factory worker, at fifty years old, doesn't feel supported in immediately going to school for two years; there are kids to feed. For those who advocate basic income, perhaps this kind of support for people upgrading their skills would be a good pilot project.

Future emergency tools

Even with today's rate hikes, the Bank of Canada can probably only go so far in restoring interest rates to levels that allow it to fight the next recession with that tool alone. Other tools will have to be brought into the regular toolkit.

Forward guidance and commitments to hold interest rates low seem like obvious candidates, as is an extension of a low-rate policy. The use of special programs to relieve market stress in some parts of fixed-income trading is a traditional "lender of last resort" feature, but it opens debate about conflict of interest or selective bailouts. The Bank could do far more to lay out guidelines of transparency and fair dealing when buying corporate and provincial bonds in the future.

Quantitative easing seems like a prime candidate for the semi-regular toolkit, yet the benefits are still unclear, and so are the exit strategies. This too needs more clarification. Should the Bank really have unlimited and indefinite power to buy government bonds? Shouldn't there be rules about how long the policy can be in place before it's wound up?

One final frontier we have yet to test in Canada is negative interest rates. I don't see this as a good option because it would scare the public, and it hasn't been the lifesaving option as advertised. No nation has emerged from a funk because of negative interest rates. Without a time limitation, or a limit on how negative you would go, this could be a trap.

What will be interesting for Canada is, given that we have safe banks, we avoided a banking and housing crash, and we avoided the use of QE in 2008, whether we can get out of these emergency policies at all, and whether we can rebuild the clearance space to cut rates significantly at the next crisis.

Should the Bank be more transparent?

I can be brief here. Canada has been doing inflation targeting longer and better than most other nations, so it's unclear how being more transparent would lead to a better outcome.

Canada was second after New Zealand to adopt an inflation target, making us first among the G7 major economies. Eventually, many other nations got on board. Canada has also been more successful, especially since 2008, in getting inflation on target. This success seems a strong argument for avoiding change. More transparency, such as publishing the minutes of interest-rate meetings, won't make the Bank's end results better, and it would be more of an illusion of transparency. There may be more transparent central banks, but they aren't doing a better job in terms of the results, nor is any central bank reviled or admired because of one stance or the other.

When it comes to real transparency, one example given is the hiring of Governors. The process happens behind closed doors, with the Bank's board of directors providing a nomination to the Finance Minister for approval. The government has moved some of its hiring for key positions and appointments to the Senate, for example, more transparent, and sometimes parliamentary hearings are held to review nominations. In the case of a Bank of Canada Governor, I sense it's a job that doesn't come open very often and there is a small pool of candidates who might meet all of the qualifications. Opening the process to public scrutiny risks driving off good candidates. Again, it's a question of whether there's a problem here. Canada has never had a terrible Governor, so I'm not sure what benefit would come from this.

On publishing meeting minutes, my concern is more basic. Canada has done arguably the best job of meeting its mandate among major central banks. If anyone can explain how to markedly improve that record by publishing minutes, I could be persuaded.

But really, given the regular press conferences and speeches after other decisions, who wants minutes to write up and think about weeks later? Minutes could also give rise to an unhealthy groupthink in the meetings—deputies might not want to express off-consensus views. The media would likely give the most oxygen to the most off-base ideas brought up in a meeting.

Given the Bank of Canada Act says only the Governor sets policy, and they say they work by consensus, publishing minutes could open up perceptions of deep divisions on policy. That would raise needless doubts about the path the Bank of Canada is taking.

Finally, the U.S. central bank publishes minutes of its meetings, and I'm not sure they are widely beneficial for the public.

Part of me thinks Deputy Governors should be allowed to give speeches with their own views and not just the consensus. Being able to speak more freely in public would be better than having their views dribble out in minutes that would likely keep their names anonymous.

The Bank of Canada will start publishing meeting summaries in 2023, based on the results of a review of its transparency practices by the International Monetary Fund. Time will tell if they are indeed appreciated by the public or if they add to productive debate.

Economics so White (and Male)

Let me offer you one disappointing memory of financial markets and inclusion. I was in New York to watch an investor conference where a senior Bank official was speaking. The Bank of Canada official, a woman, spoke later in the conference, after a panel of several men. I was in a big snazzy room surrounded mostly by the elite young men, the traders who needed to know these things.

As soon as the panel discussion ended and the Bank of Canada official began to speak, the entire long row of young professionals behind me got up to leave, and they made a fair amount of noise and commotion. While it could have been that they had been denied even a late lunch or they had other meetings to get to, it looked crass. For investors who are known for hanging on a central bank's every word, this was a rare chance to hear directly from someone important, so it just didn't add up.

As I began writing this book, the Bank had no women or visible minorities on its Governing Council, which sets interest rates. By the time I finished this draft, they had appointed two women to Governing Council. Official Ottawa, in general, is still too white and male.

When I was in university in the 1990s the number of women in economics courses dropped off dramatically, even after first year. And kept dropping off. Given the material, and the many very solid math and English students in my classes, I couldn't figure it out. Economics has been gripped in recent years by tales of a hostile or unfeeling environment that is very conformist. It's a shame. Much more work needs to be done to develop solid candidates from university through to the professional ranks.

Low for long interest rates

We have been in a period of low interest rates for quite a while. Yes, interest rates are rising, but as I've pointed out, it doesn't appear that rates will move back up above five percent for a long time. Where does that leave monetary policy when it's mostly a cycle of low and moderate interest rates, and policy makers are always at risk of being stuck at the "zero lower bound" with no room to cut further in a downturn?

I calculated that, under Poloz, the pause in interest rates was the longest since after World War II. Back then, policy making was very different, and it was partly dictated by the need for stability around war bonds that Canadians intended to cash in for fair value.

While central bankers create the illusion that today's policy regime is eternal, changes always come. Given the emergence of emergency tools to compensate for the low-for-long interest rates, will a regular inflation target and interest rates as the key tools of monetary policy last for another couple of decades? If the world again shifts with something like a digital currency, even one controlled by the Bank, that could easily upend the financial system, the transmission of monetary policy, and perhaps even the economy itself.

The dominant forces now seem to be the dangerous gravity of low-for-long interest rates, curbing market bubbles, and bigger changes in the nature of work, population, productivity, and global competition. We can't turn our backs on regulating inflation, but I would suggest some of the older tools of moral suasion, and perhaps some control over destabilizing financial market trends could be due for a comeback.

Simply put, the Bank of Canada has never insisted the buck stops with them for anything other than a war on inflation, which it largely won in the 1990s. It seems something more imaginative could be accomplished. When you look at risks from climate change and the housing boom, the Bank could become more of a sentinel on emerging risks.

Some concluding thoughts

The period between 2000 and 2022 has been defined by both the longest pause in interest rates since World War II, and by a long line of miserable events, from Y2K and the dot-com boom to the 9/11 terror attacks and SARS, BSE, devastating floods in Ottawa and British Columbia, heatwaves, years of fractious trade talks with the Trump administration, and finally, the Covid-19 pandemic. And the period is ending with the fastest inflation since the early 1980s.

Most economic models of the economy are designed for smooth waves of forces such as inflation and economic growth. No one in charge can really know what shock might reset consumer and business behaviour, and create truly destabilizing events like the U.S. housing and banking crash of 2008-09. What is remarkable is that the Bank of Canada has been the only Group of Seven central bank to meet its two percent target most of the time. And this in a nation known as a "small, open economy" and a "price taker" for most of its major commodity exports into world markets, or in other words, a nation that isn't always in full control of its economic destiny.

How did we do it? Perhaps having a single mandate of two percent inflation prevented perceptions that there would be cheating on the inflation target, or perhaps the dramatic swings in the Canadian dollar sent a clearer signal about price changes. Over time, I also feel that having eight fixed meeting dates and clear cycle of preparations around meetings helped policy makers step back from day-to-day events and come up with thoughtful decisions rather than making hasty announcements.

It's been a credit to the Bank and its staff that they have guided the economy through so many shocks, and a credit to Canadians that the economy has been so resilient and flexible. No one could have predicted that we would not go into the same recession the U.S. after the 9/11 attacks. Or that, rather than facing long-term economic damage, the economy would set a historic low for unemployment, only months after the omicron wave of Covid passed.

Canada managed to miss some major pitfalls, such as the U.S. recessions, Brexit in the U.K., and the political and economic populism seen from Hungary to the Philippines. It may be fair to remember that, in the 1990s in Canada, we faced down challenges from a damaging recession that exposed a lack of competitiveness; Paul Martin's "hell or high water" budget, which steered us away from being frozen out of global bond markets; the Quebec referendum; and the rise and fall of some anti-immigration sentiment. It was during that time in the early 1990s that the inflation target was created by the Bank of Canada, arguably the most important foundation of policy since the central bank was created in the depths of the Great Depression in the 1930s.

But the longer history of monetary policy shows that what works today may not work tomorrow. The Bank has moved through phases of "moral suasion," fixed exchange rates, a global reliance on seeing the money supply as the best guidepost of policy and inflation pressures, and global bank deregulation and its aftermath. While I can't see any catalyst for moving away from a clear inflation target, and neither can most Canadians, there could be a time when either a major shift in the underlying economy or a massive shock requires a change in thinking.

Just as commercial banks since 2008 have faced "stress tests" to see what damage the banking or housing system can withstand, and too often the results are blandly reassuring, the Bank of Canada must be prepared to make bigger changes if the economy shifts. Even a continued passing grade is no guarantee of future success.

One possible catalyst for change would be if inflation gets stuck at a very high or very low level, at which point repeating the wish to get it back to two percent no longer has the same credibility. (As of late 2022, although inflation is quite high, there are signs it's slowing down again and not stuck at eight percent). To be clear, though, calls to raise the inflation target aren't satisfying because that would largely ratify rising prices. And at this point, a debate in the other direction, lowering the inflation target, seems unrealistic.

Canada has also skated by so far on its massive levels of household debt. If there is another crash, that will challenge the idea that the Bank of Canada should have held interest rates low for so long and shifted responsibility for essentially free money to others. The announcement during Covid that everyone could take a six-month extension or "payment holiday" on their mortgages during the pandemic; the very existence of such a policy admits that Canadians don't have the savings required to cover financial emergencies. But apparently, many could still obtain a mortgage for a house. Finally, the rise of digital money could be corrosive to the effectiveness of monetary policy.

In the next fifteen years, the Bank of Canada will turn one hundred years old. The title of this book is focused on good times and bad. While we should debate the potential for big change and improvement, there is also a danger in tinkering with what works. The bottom line is that the Bank of Canada has been a source of stability, working mostly in the background, over this time period. Which is what you want from a central bank.

CHAPTER SIXTEEN

Mostly for the Pros: Closely reading what the Bank says

Reading Bank of Canada interest-rate decisions

One of the biggest jobs of the financial press is to interpret clues from the Bank of Canada on potential interest-rate changes in every speech, interest rate decision, and quarterly economic forecast (known as the Monetary Policy Report (MPR)). Small changes can immediately change the value of Canada's foreign exchange rate, and the prices of bonds and other securities. While reporters get speeches embargoed in advance lock-ups at the Bank of Canada, and an hour or so to read them over, it can still be difficult to figure out new language, throw-away lines, and real shifts in thinking.

The interest rate decisions are on one page with perhaps 500 words, so there isn't that much, in volume terms, to think over. For investors and journalists, the news is often at the end, so it's a bit like finding out who the murderer was at the end of a mystery novel. After finding the line at the end saying what the Bank intends to do next, you can go back and read the context of how we got to where we are now.

The most important thing is sifting out statements about the economy's past, and past Bank actions, and focusing on what they are saying about the future trends. Secondly, it's important to pay less attention to references to uncertainty, since things are always uncertain.

In more normal times, another exercise that has often paid off was reading a decision and counting the number of positive and negative references to parts of the economy. There were times when interest rates were unchanged, but almost every comment was negative (or positive), which was a hidden clue about the Bank's attitude.

Also, doing a word count on the decision statement told me a lot. If the statement was short, it meant the Bank had a confident handle on the economy. If it was longer, it often meant they had more things to study and less conviction about where to go. Statements that took up just one side of a sheet of paper were generally confident; those that ran to the other side suggested more worries.

Above all, the Bank has a single mandate of keeping inflation at two percent. You can't get carried away by a new phrase on investment or something similar unless it ties to the inflation story. Often, people misinterpret these decisions because they focus on side issues over the mandate. If you don't come away with a view of what the Bank of Canada thinks about inflation, you have become distracted and missed the point. The Bank can say they are optimistic about ten different things, but if they still say inflation risks are to the downside, that is probably what their policy will have to address.

I always bring in a copy of the previous few statements and look for ideas and phrases that have been added or dropped. This often signals economic turning points. It's also smart to have read over everything the Bank has said in the weeks since the last decision to see if any new comments since then are amplified in the new rate decision. Also helpful is to be prepared with all the market research to know what investors are expecting to happen and what would be a surprise. Even reading my own stories over the prior few weeks was useful for jogging my memory for key ideas.

Some statements do make references that are quite rare and deserve outside attention, even if they are very brief. The Bank doesn't often directly comment on the value of the Canadian dollar, on the potential for a recession, or that inflation will be outside its one to three percent target band. When those words show up, it's more serious.

Of course, it's also less common to have a direct line in the decisions saying interest rates will rise or fall, and you should take them at their word. In more normal times, these references are rare and the Bank can give some more subtle signals about rates moving up potentially over a course of three or six months.

Reading Bank Speeches and Monetary Policy Reports

When it comes to speeches, they are often pretty long, and helpfully, the biggest clue, if there is one, is often at the end of the speech. We often gloss over most of the remarks in the first three-quarters of the speech. This is where the financial press diverges from other media, who will focus their coverage on the bulk of the remarks about the job market or the housing market, for example. Investors generally just want to know if interest rates are rising or falling.

This coverage is what pays the bills for the financial press.

The hard part in reading these documents is not to overreach. Sometimes a speech really is about the past or about a side topic for markets, and it's best to not overdo it, even though your competitors might write a longer story. There is usually one investor in the crowd willing to tell you that a given speech has a major hidden meaning. This requires some common sense; a lecture to university students about the job market probably should not be over-interpreted for hidden investment clues.

In the quarterly Monetary Policy Reports, I pore over the economic forecast tables almost as much as the text itself. It's important to start by looking at the big picture of whether economic growth and inflation are being revised up or down, suggesting that interest rates may rise or fall.

Given that the Bank has a two percent inflation target, how soon we get to that level can be very important.

It's also important to look at the underlying details that led to the total forecast for growth. Is it being led by housing, exports, business investment, or government spending? For most of the last decade, the composition of growth has been led by consumer spending and rarely by business spending.

The times in which exports and investment take a bigger role are a sign of high optimism.

During the pandemic, of course, the specific economic numbers are less important than the Bank's overall assessment of dangers to the outlook from lockdowns or global inflation risks.

In normal times, when the economy and monetary policy are running fairly smoothly, there will be few major revisions to the Bank's economic forecast. In those times, when the Bank shifts to make larger changes to its view on exports, inflation, or consumer spending, for example, pay closer attention.

What I have found helpful is to have some knowledge of what private economists are predicting for the economic outlook. If they see a housing correction, or an export boom, for example, it can be a useful contrast with the Bank of Canada's overall story. If there are some big disagreements, it's wise to step back and ask what the Bank of Canada would have to do if it's overall story could turn out to be wrong. The Bank's views, long after the global financial crisis, that investment and exports might take off is an example; since that took a long time to unfold, it might have been easy to guess that the Bank would have a much harder time raising interest rates than it wanted to.

The Monetary Policy Report can also be quickly summed up in the first section on the domestic economy. Some officials have suggested that the opening section is almost an executive summary of the interest-rate meetings. For someone wanting a quick read of the Bank's thinking, you could skim that first section and have things fairly well in hand.

The other thing I always read closely is the language at the end of the Monetary Policy Report on the balance of risks to inflation. Firstly, given the Bank's mandate to bring inflation to target within two years, which is a pretty long runway, if they ever say the risks are unbalanced, that's a big clue that rates are likely to rise or fall. An economy that's at risk of overheating, for example, through such a long period likely needs higher interest rates. In normal times, the Bank confidently says the risks are balanced, but if there are other things of concern going on, it's another chance to think about whether the Bank will need to play catch-up later.

The Monetary Policy Reports are also quite long, so one shortcut is to look over the headlines of each section. They represent a CliffNotes summary of the main ideas.

All that said, it's a poor journalist who doesn't read every word for that key nugget of truth in a speech or economic forecast paper.

I have also learned not to ignore the footnotes when they appear, because sometimes they include an interesting data trend that's led to some good follow up stories.

While these are the places to get your top ideas for the headline and start of your story, you still have to read the whole thing for backup. Often, the rest of your story is built on the two or three interesting statistics scattered through the thirty or forty pages of the MPR or speech.

Remember the single inflation mandate

What I keep in mind with all the reports I read is that the Bank of Canada has a single mandate of keeping inflation at two percent. Any language talking about inflation trends or risks has to be part of the story, even when the dollar is flying high or oil exports are crashing. If the inflation outlook is little changed you can perhaps skip it. If you've written a story that implies the economy is really strong, and you have a line in there saying inflation is modest, you have to rethink what you're doing.

The inflation rate is also a good guidepost to compare with the Bank's key interest rate, as a way of getting inside the heads of policy makers. If the two are very different from each other these days, it's a sign of how much of a risk they are taking either overheating or tightening up on the economy.

Economists talk about a "real" interest rate, which is the interest rate minus the rate of inflation or inflation expectations. If the Bank's key rate is 0.25 percent, that is historically low and a lot of stimulus. But if the inflation rate falls below one percent as it did in 2020, then the actual amount of stimulus isn't as strong. On the other hand, if inflation was at two percent and the interest rate was 0.25 percent, that would be like pouring gasoline on a fire, and the Bank of Canada must think hard about whether that situation is sustainable. Ideally, there is a "neutral" interest rate that keeps the economy on the level, and policy makers do think about that balance.

One reason the Bank of Canada began raising interest rates so quickly in 2022 was that the interest rate started the year at 0.25 percent and inflation started moving up well past the five percent mark. This was a clear sign that we needed interest rates to at least get back to neutral to restore economic balance.

Usually there is a single keyword

For the volume of words journalists read through, it's often a single keyword that captures the whole story. I know central bankers decry this, even as they sometimes play into it. Because central bankers are also famous for speaking in befuddled phrases, the media has an important role in translating it into something that's easier to understand. (When central banks worldwide said inflation was "transitory" as the economy was rebounding from Covid, that said a lot, and when central banks said they were "resolute" in bringing inflation back down, that was also the dominant idea.)

Governor David Dodge made waves in markets when he answered an audience question—what do you mean by changing "monetary stimulus"—he replied with the obvious, saying it meant changing interest rates. Markets hailed this as a beacon of clarity, and it's an example of how even what may seem like small language changes in the central bank can be very helpful to the public.

While some shifts are significant, I think we shouldn't overdo it. If a Governor has a message, it will be given. Anything else is a secondary consideration or fumbled wording.

Former Governor Stephen Poloz's view of setting policy was a solid one. He said there are "zones" of economic performance, and the broad economy is not a racing motorcycle capable of hairpin turns. There is little point in fine-tuning an economy in most cases, or using language that suggests very subtle changes. In my time, investors obsessed for months over pet phrases like "tightening bias" and "falling behind the curve" or "sending the market a message"—turns of phrase that really meant very little.

The difference between a brilliant and failed markets story on a Bank of Canada event is finding the one phrase out of five or six that really shows a change in thinking about where interest rates are heading. And choosing the most relevant one is tough. No matter how smart or experienced you are, the market is bigger than you. Your competitors capture the best ideas better than you do. Sometimes the phrase you thought was just an obvious restatement of what the Governor has been saying for six months sparks a dollar rally and your boss wants to speak to the twit that put the re-written coverage an hour behind the competition. You feel shame, you tell yourself the market is crazy and wrong. And you go back and do it all again in a week or so. Sometimes readers will email notes, sometimes even to your bosses, saying you overplayed a point and have it wrong. There is real pressure behind this. Sometimes, those readers themselves have staked a bet in the markets they need to come true, so their views are sometimes a bit skewed. You do your best. And in most cases, your bosses back you up.

Reading federal budgets

The other big thing financial journalists do is read federal budgets. These are massive documents, but my approach was to keep the focus narrow on key investment messages. There are dozens of political reporters in Ottawa who can craft stories for a wider audience.

That said, I read the speech first to see the main idea of the budget's spirit. That is helpful, but what makes the story is in the first couple of tables summarizing the actual budget numbers. From there you often see the contrast between the story the government is telling about fiscal responsibility and what is actually happening. While governments do use some tricks to draw attention away from what they are doing, ultimately the figures on revenue, spending, and debt costs can't hide the truth.

In other words, stick to the numbers around deficits and debt. Compare those to the historical trend and the deficit and debt compared to the size of the economy. By the time you put those in proper context, you don't have time for much else.

You do have to be aware of tricks played to hide spending, like special funds or calling things "investments." Accounting rules change, so today's figures aren't historically comparable. Also, given that a government lasts four years, tops, before an election, it's best to focus most attention on the dollars that are going out the door this year and next. Everything thing else can be paved over in the next budget and never happen. Yet most media stories play up five-year plans and projections that are truly irrelevant. Another thing to keep in mind is that Finance Ministers and Prime Ministers often don't last five years, and if they do, it's not because they carefully finished off a spending plan they set up five years ago.

Often the main challenge is that governments now often leak the narrative they want to promote in advance of the budget, moving you away from hidden truths. Before reporters see the full budget document, we're told the plan is for a "housing budget," a "climate budget," and so on. It's our job to find the whole picture.

Another challenge is that governments often use the budget to shift blame for costs or deficits onto the previous government, and so on.

Unfunded promises are also a major issue today. Think of fighter jets, indigenous measures, or climate change adaptation. The projects that haven't been paid for should be woven into the budget stories.

Budgets must also be read against the economic backdrop. Governments are tempted to inflate economic growth to help them make programs seem affordable. Or fiddle with assumptions about interest rates and the cost of carrying debt, inflation, and so on. It's good to read up in advance to figure out what economists expect the economy to do, and see if there are any big gaps in the budget.

Why is this important? Governments that head towards going broke face constraints. Cities generally can't run deficits or the province blocks them, and it's the same for school boards, health care boards, and so on. Provinces have limited scope for carrying debt before it eats into their program spending. Even the federal government faced a "debt wall" in the late 1980s and early 1990s; they knew their credit rating was being cut and that global investors would stop lending the money they needed. This made Paul Martin Prime Minister, with his "hell or high water" budget.

Finally, while budgets are always very large documents, more recently they have become "omnibus bills," including many things that have little to do with accounting for where the money is going. It's important to find those nuggets of new programs that aren't being advertised, but are buried deep in the document. For investors, I have always pored over the annual debt strategy to look for new types of bonds being sold and other changes of the terms of debt auctions.

Sadly, most reporters don't have the time to go back and follow up on all the things in a budget beyond a day or two. And it's impossible to read a 250-page document in one day. Despite the challenges, it's important to go back to the document over the next few days and read the parts you had to skim over for nuggets.

Reading too much into the Bank

There are a couple of views on how the Bank works that I think are over-blown. Investors often say the Bank of Canada is much more likely to move rates in the four (of eight) meetings per year that also result in a Monetary Policy Report. That seems only partly true, because while Bank of Canada officials can have more confidence about their decisions when they have a fresh quarterly economic forecast, they wouldn't schedule eight meetings a year if they only intended to use four of them. Also, when you look at the crises of 2008 and 2020, it was clear that a good chunk of the action wasn't even scheduled, let alone held over for the "real" decision every quarter.

The media has also occasionally played some parlour games around the private meetings between Governors and Finance Ministers. The Bank of Canada Act itself states the Governor and minister should consult regularly to avoid stepping on each other. Makes perfect sense. While they were always kept private, I gathered some access to information request documents suggesting it was a quick phone call every couple of weeks, meetings if they were at a G7 or G20, or sometimes in person. How can you run an economy if you don't know what the other big policy maker is doing? More to the point, it could be disaster if the Governor and Finance Minister made seemingly contradictory comments about Canada's economy on the same day. Yet the media and investors ran stories for years about any hint of a meeting as if it was a special emergency. The same thing happens with stories about Bank of Canada meetings with financial firm CEOs, which happen once or twice a year. Again, imagine a world in which the banks and central bank CEOs never met.

Finally, news reporting sometimes gets carried away with the idea that swings in the job market or the housing market will lead to some kind of direct policy response. I can barely remember any case in which one market in distress led to an overall policy shift. As stated many times in this book, the inflation rate is *the* mandate.

SELECTED READINGS

The Worldly Philosophers: The Lives, Times, and Ideas of the Great Economic Thinkers, by Robert L. Heilbroner

A Mathematician Reads the Newspaper, by John Allen Paulos

Empire of Cotton: A Global History, by Sven Beckert

Canadian War Economics, edited by J.F. Parkinson

Alexander Hamilton, by Ron Chernow

Fast Food Nation, by Eric Schlosser

Liar's Poker, by Michael Lewis

Capitalism, Socialism and Democracy, by Joseph A. Schumpeter

Titan: The Life of John D. Rockefeller, by Ron Chernow

The Prosperous Few and the Restless Many, by Noam Chomsky

The Bank of Canada of James Elliott Coyne: Challenges, Confrontation, and Change, by James Powell

The Wealth of Nations, Books I-III, by Adam Smith

> "It is not from the benevolence of the butcher, the brewer, or the baker, that we expect our dinner, but from their regard to their own interest. We address ourselves, not to

their humanity but to their self-love, and never talk to them of our own necessities, but of their advantages."

Capital, Volume 1, by Karl Marx

"Capital, therefore, is not only the command over labour, as Adam Smith thought. It is essentially the command over unpaid labour."

Lombard Street: A Description of the Money Market, by Walter Bagehot

Genghis Khan and the Making of the Modern World, by Jack Weatherford

In Your Best Interest: The Ultimate Guide to the Canadian Bond Market, by W.H. "Hank" Cunningham

What I Learned About Politics: Inside the Rise—and Collapse—of Nova Scotia's NDP Government, by Graham Steele

Graham Towers and His Times, by Douglas H. Fullerton

Citizens Irving: K.C. Irving and His Legacy, by John DeMont

Cod: A Biography of the Fish That Changed the World, by Mark Kurlansky

The Belly of Paris, by Emile Zola

The Power Broker: Robert Moses and the Fall of New York, by Robert A. Caro

The Politics of Public Spending in Canada, by Donald J. Savoie

Maestro: Greenspan's Fed and the American Boom, by Bob Woodward

The Age of Turbulence: Adventures in a New World, by Alan Greenspan

Secrets of the Temple: How the Federal Reserve Runs the Country, by William Greider

Banker to the Poor: Micro-Lending and the Battle Against World Poverty, by Muhammad Yunus

The Mystery of Capital: Why Capitalism Triumphs in the West and Fails Everywhere Else, by Hernando de Soto

ABOUT ME

Born in Halifax, Nova Scotia, in 1975, and raised in Dartmouth across the harbour, I delivered *The Daily News* and *Chronicle Herald* to earn money as a kid. Writing began for me when my high school English teacher, Ms. Bowlby, press-ganged me into overseeing a newspaper—really just three pieces of paper stapled together from the school printer, and sold for a quarter. I wrote funny horoscopes, and only later, some half serious news stories about some strife with teachers.

My first economics class was in high school under Mr. Gillis, a true Cape Bretoner. I did well enough to follow my older brother, Scott, to Mount Allison University, the best school I've ever gone to. Go there if you can. There I worked at the student newspaper and ended up being a news editor. My economics marks were good enough for me to talk my way into a scholarship at the University of Toronto, and I wanted to build my expertise in economics before turning to journalism. I believe in "write what you know."

Western University lost my journalism school application when they moved offices, and refused to review my application when I asked why I had no response, leading to a panicky forty-eight hours before Columbia University in New York accepted my application, (which I had mostly seen as a lark, to a place I would never go). Columbia sent me to the Bronx for most of the year, where I interviewed a convicted murder and the mother of his victim, snuck my way into a Head Start (early childhood learning for poor children) class to see how some of the poorest immigrant families in America were faring, and spent many hours on the D train to the southeast Bronx where I was often the only white person on the train. I wrote about the urban culture of new shoe releases and the value of gold jewelry in the Black and Latino communities. I had a paid internship with Bloomberg in Washington lined up before I finished school. I went to work at five a.m., and distributed faxes to one hundred news desks, based on my best guess of who covered what. I witnessed the Y2K bug and the shocking Clinton impeachment. Little did I know then that the echoes of the internet, questionable information, and impeachment would return to political life in America. I was offered a job at Bloomberg's Toronto office, covering bonds and the dollar, and it was in Toronto that I met Amanda, my wife and the mother of our two daughters. We eventually moved to Ottawa, where I still cover economics, filing on just about every budget, election, and crisis you can imagine, and from every province and territory except Nunavut. (Hopefully I will get there someday.) For the last few years, I have been the Canada correspondent for *Market News International*, where I also do some editing and help with Federal Reserve coverage.